COMPILED BY

JENNIFER BARDOT

GROWTH • RESILIENCE

SUCCESSFUL

Entrepreneurs

WITH

G.R.I.T.®

INTENTION • TENACITY

Entrepreneurs juggle the demands of business, family, and personal ambition—
often stumbling, but always rising with resilience and determination.
This book celebrates their hard-earned wisdom, honoring the growth, grit,
and lessons that shape their journey toward success.

Successful Entrepreneurs with G.R.I.T.
MDC Press

Published by **MDC Press**, St. Louis, MO
Copyright ©2025
All rights reserved.

All contributing authors to this anthology have submitted their chapters to an editing process and have accepted the recommendations of the editors at their own discretion. All authors have approved their chapters prior to publication.

Cover, Interior Design, and Project Management:
  Davis Creative Publishing, DavisCreativePublishing.com

Writing Coaches and Editors: Kristy Barton and Jason Meinershagen
Compilation by Jennifer Bardot

Publisher's Cataloging-in-Publication
Names: Bardot, Jennifer, compiler.
Title: Successful entrepreneurs with G.R.I.T. / compiled by Jennifer Bardot.
Other titles: Successful entrepreneurs with Growth, Resilience, Intention, Tenacity
Description: St. Louis, MO : MDC Press, [2025] | Series: G.R.I.T.
Identifiers: LCCN: 2025907528 | ISBN: 9798991897020 (paperback) | 9798991897037 (ebook)
Subjects: LCSH: Businesspeople--Psychology--Literary collections. | Businesspeople--Psychology--Anecdotes. | Entrepreneurship--Psychological aspects--Literary collections. | Entrepreneurship--Psychological aspects--Anecdotes. | Success in business--Psychological aspects--Literary collections. | Success in business--Psychological aspects--Anecdotes. | Resilience (Personality trait)--Literary collections. | Resilience (Personality trait)--Anecdotes. | Perseverance (Ethics)--Literary collections. | Perseverance (Ethics)--Anecdotes. | LCGFT: Anecdotes. | BISAC: BUSINESS & ECONOMICS / Motivational. | BIOGRAPHY & AUTOBIOGRAPHY / Business. | SELF-HELP / Personal Growth / General.
Classification: LCC: HB615 .S83 2025 | DDC: 658.4/21--dc23

Dedication

I dedicate this book
to my boys, whose love
gives me purpose
and resilience.

To all the entrepreneurs
who have dared to leap—
channeling their passion into
leadership and building
something of their own—
you inspire this journey.

TABLE OF CONTENTS

Title Authors

Continued on next page

Additional Authors

In Memorium

*Dedicated to the life
and entrepreneurial spirit
of Lisa York.*

*We can only aspire to live a life like Lisa's,
which touched so many and left them
all the better for knowing her.*

*The ripple effect of the lives
she has changed will last forever.*

We are grateful and blessed to have known her.

Lisa York
December 2, 1963 — May 5, 2025

Foreword

Entrepreneurship is not for the faint of heart.

It asks everything of you—your energy, your clarity, your conviction—and then it asks for more. It demands courage when the future is uncertain, persistence when the odds are stacked against you, and resourcefulness when the path forward isn't obvious. But if there's one word that sums up what it truly takes to build something from nothing, it's this: **G.R.I.T.**

Growth. Resilience. Intention. Tenacity.

That's what you'll find in the pages of this powerful book.

In this special edition of the *G.R.I.T.* series, Jennifer Bardot has assembled a remarkable group of entrepreneurs—twenty-six bold business owners who've said "yes" to the challenge of turning vision into value. These are not sanitized, fairy-tale versions of success. These are honest, real, vulnerable accounts of what it actually looks like to *do the work*—to bet on yourself, to fail forward, and to keep building even when no one's watching.

These entrepreneurs have navigated uncertainty, rejection, pivots, and pressure. They've learned the lessons only the journey can teach—how to stretch resources, build trust, follow your gut, and stay rooted in your "why" when everything else is shifting. Each of their stories is a masterclass in possibility, driven by purpose and powered by sheer determination.

As someone who has spent my career helping founders and executives scale their businesses—from early-stage ideas to market-dominating companies—I know firsthand what it takes to make it. Success is not just about strategy or funding. It's about mindset. Momentum. Mission. And perhaps most importantly, the ability to keep showing up even when things get messy, hard, or uncertain.

Because let's face it—entrepreneurship *is* messy. And it's supposed to be.

It's a constant dance between vision and execution, risk and reward, confidence and humility. And there's no single blueprint for getting it "right." What works for one founder may not work for another. But the common thread—the real secret sauce—is grit.

Grit is what carries you when the plan changes.

Grit is what fuels your belief when the results are delayed.

Grit is what reminds you that building something meaningful isn't about going fast—it's about going deep.

Grit is about being a show-up person. Every. Day.

That's what makes this book such a gift.

Each story is more than a snapshot—it's a spark. A reminder that no matter where you are on your journey, you're not alone. You're a part of a growing community of dreamers, doers, and difference-makers who have chosen the road less traveled. And while the path may be steep, the view from the top is worth every step.

What I love most about this book is its diversity—not just of industries, but of backgrounds, styles, and business stages. These entrepreneurs bring unique perspectives to the table, yet they're united by a shared commitment to impact and innovation. Their courage is contagious. Their wisdom hard-won. And their willingness to share their stories is nothing short of generous.

Jennifer Bardot has once again created something that goes beyond inspiration—she's created *connection*. She's amplified the voices of entrepreneurs who are in the trenches, doing the work, building the future. That kind of storytelling matters. It builds bridges. It breaks down silos. And it reminds us that behind every successful business is a human being who chose to believe in something bigger than themselves.

So, whether you're a seasoned entrepreneur, an aspiring founder, or someone simply curious about what it takes to build a business from the ground up, this book is for you. Let it challenge you. Let it comfort you. Let it call you to action.

Because the world needs more builders. More people willing to bring their ideas to life—not in pursuit of perfection, but in service of purpose.

To the twenty-six incredible entrepreneurs featured in this book: Thank you for your bravery, your honesty, transparency, and your leadership. You've chosen the harder road, and in doing so, you've made it easier for the next generation to follow in your footsteps.

To Jennifer: Thank you for being a fearless curator of real stories and real people. Your work lights a path for so many others.

And to the reader: May these stories ignite something in you. May they remind you that your dreams are valid, your voice is needed, and your grit is your greatest advantage.

The future belongs to those bold enough to create it.

Let's get to work.

Laura Burkemper

CEO | SCALEBLAZER™ | *Startup to Grownup*™

Business & Brand Strategist | Investor

Best-Selling Author| Broadway Show Producer

Helping visionary leaders' position for **Investment | Scale | Sale**™

Laura Burkemper is the business and brand strategist behind some of today's most innovative and influential companies. As CEO of SCALEBLAZER™, she empowers visionary leaders and celebrity brands to turn bold ideas into market-dominating companies. With a global client portfolio and eighty emerging business investments, she is a leader in positioning businesses for Investment | Scale | Sale™.

A trailblazer in Investable Storytelling™, Building Brand Capital™, and Negotiating Better Outcomes™, Laura's insights have been featured across CNBC, FOX Business, ABC, CBS, NBC, *Essence, Us Weekly, The Business Journal*, and NPR.

Best-selling co-author of *Empathy & Understanding in Business* with FBI negotiator Chris Voss, Laura illustrates how a go-giver mindset drives extraordinary business success. In 2024, she took storytelling to Broadway, making her debut as a producer of *When My Soul Speaks*, featuring L.A.'s global motivational powerhouse Lisa Nichols.

Laura's leadership journey includes pivotal roles at Coca-Cola, McDonald's, and Express Scripts, where she translated strategic vision into business, brand, and growth strategies that delivered measurable results. She earned an MBA in International Business from Saint Louis University, where she has taught entrepreneurship in its top-ranked program since 2010. She holds a Bachelor of Science in Business Administration from the University of Missouri-St. Louis, a Certificate in Negotiation

Mastery from Harvard Business School Online, and serves as a Harvard Business Review Advisory Council member.

Overall, Laura is dedicated to growing businesses, empowering visionary leaders, and fueling the entrepreneurial mindset!

Please scan the QR code to connect with this author.

Preface

I grew up knowing I wanted to be an entrepreneur. From a young age, I was drawn to the rhythm of business—the conversations, the challenges, the hustle. I watched my family run our business, observed my uncle manage his company, and listened closely as close friends shared stories from their family enterprises. Business ownership wasn't just an idea; it was part of my world.

Still, despite my early exposure and deep interest, I struggled with confidence. I wasn't sure I had what it took to lead, to build something from the ground up, or to be taken seriously as a business owner. But life has a way of nudging us toward our purpose. What started as a side hustle—something small, something just for me—quickly grew into something bigger. It evolved into a business, then into a calling.

Along the way, I made every mistake imaginable. I've learned that success isn't just about big wins or picture-perfect plans—it's about consistency, discipline, clarity, and the courage to keep going, especially when things get hard.

This book is for the dreamers, the side hustlers, the legacy builders, the founders, and the thriving business owners. It's for anyone who's ever wondered, *"What if I tried going out on my own?"* Within these pages, you'll find real stories, honest lessons, and practical advice for navigating the entrepreneurial journey.

Above all, this book is about GRIT—**Growth, Resilience, Intention, and Tenacity**—the qualities that every successful entrepreneur must develop and nurture. Whether you're just getting started or already running a successful venture, I hope this book encourages you, challenges you, and reminds you that with GRIT, anything is possible.

Jennifer Bardot, MA, MS
Founder of G.R.I.T.

G.R.I.T.®

Jennifer Bardot

Leading with G.R.I.T.

When I think of successful entrepreneurs, I think about how each of us uniquely defines success. To me, being an entrepreneur carries risks—but also incredible rewards. As a mother, it gives me the freedom to shape my schedule and be present for my family. But more than that, becoming an entrepreneur has been about proving to myself—and to my family—that I am capable of leading with vision, purpose, and strength.

I come from a proud legacy of business ownership. For four generations, my family has operated businesses, beginning in 1933 within the commercial construction industry. By working within that legacy and for my uncle's company, I gained invaluable experience in customer service, business development, and partnership building. Back then, a handshake sealed a deal, and your word meant everything. While times have changed, I still carry those values with me today.

So, how do you define success?

It took me years to take the leap into entrepreneurship. The fear of risk held me back. But even in my early twenties, I caught a glimpse of the grit it takes not only to start a business, but also to sustain one. At 21, I launched "Premier Cleaning Services, LLC." I went all in—knocking on doors, creating marketing strategies, and assembling a team. I also learned hard lessons. When others began offering similar services and undercutting my rates, I felt exposed and discouraged. But that experience set me on a deeper journey. I pursued my master's degree and began the personal growth needed to become the kind of leader I aspired to be—one who leads with both heart and intention.

I've come to deeply admire business owners who boldly step into their purpose and move beyond the "what-ifs" to build something meaningful.

My father often said, "Success doesn't come without effort." That mindset stuck with me. It's helped me get through lean seasons and motivated me to grow through each new chapter.

G.R.I.T. was born in 2021, during one of the most uncertain times in recent memory. Like many of you, the challenges of the pandemic pushed me to think creatively. I saw a need to create hope through hardship and to give voice to the stories many leaders were afraid to share. The dream of building a brand rooted in courage, authenticity, and connection had been stirring in me for years, but it took courage, healing, and time to step into it fully.

When I published my first G.R.I.T. book in May 2021, I was still funding everything myself while working a corporate job. Slowly but steadily, I built the book collection, the community, the gala, the expo, and the momentum. In August 2023, on the anniversary of my second book's launch, I finally took the leap and became a full-time entrepreneur. Since then, I've published six international bestsellers—this one will mark my seventh in just five years.

Today, G.R.I.T. is a thriving brand and a community where leaders are born. We offer a membership program that supports aspiring authors, host signature events, and have expanded into a jewelry and clothing line. I also keynote on the power of G.R.I.T.—which stands for Growth, Resilience, Intention, and Tenacity.

Because of how much heart I've poured into building this brand, I decided to trademark G.R.I.T. early on. I wanted to protect what I had worked so hard to create. Along the way, I've mentored and coached countless individuals to help them share their own stories. That generosity, however, has sometimes led to confusion and even disappointment, especially when I've seen others adopt similar formats, language, or ideas.

In the past, I reacted defensively. I've since learned that while we can't control how others behave, we can control how we respond to them. Ideas may overlap, and our work may inspire people, but no one can replicate our heart, our energy, or our intention. That's where the real power lies.

The truth is that everyone has the right to create. We're all here to make our mark, and the world is big enough for us all to shine.

That realization has shifted my focus from protection to purpose. Instead of holding tightly to fear, I now anchor myself in service. My mission is to empower others to step into their light. And when that mission is rooted in authenticity, it becomes unshakable.

My family's history showed me that others may imitate, but real impact can't be duplicated. The leaders I admire most build not from ego, but from integrity. They stay grounded in their values and surround themselves with others who share the same values.

Boundaries are still important, of course. I've learned to speak up when needed and walk away when necessary. But I no longer let that distract me from my mission. As Mel Robbins said in her influential book *Let Them,* we can't control others, but we can choose to stay aligned with our vision.

Community has always mattered to me. It's why I founded an association to support the growth of others. Entrepreneurship can feel isolating, but with the right circle, we become stronger, braver, and more innovative. It's in community that our ideas sharpen, our confidence builds, and our resilience is restored.

All the lessons I've learned—through failure, missteps, and yes, even heartache—have shaped me into the leader I am today. I am far from perfect, but I am constantly evolving. And I'm more committed than ever to lifting others as I rise.

As someone with a master's in counseling, I've combined therapeutic journaling with leadership training to help others transform pain into purpose. The stories we share in G.R.I.T. are not only powerful—they're healing. They offer hope and proof that growth is always possible, even in our most broken places.

Long before I was officially an entrepreneur, I was already serving the business community. I volunteered with ITEN's pitch committee, mentored students at Lindenwood University's MENTORUP program, and offered financial insight at Washington University's Skandalaris Center. Supporting others to realize their dreams has always been part of my journey. Watching others rise fills my heart with joy.

The Value of Community

Entrepreneurship is thrilling—but also demanding. You carry the vision, the pressure, the wins, and the weight of every decision. That's why community isn't optional—it's essential.

A strong support system offers more than encouragement. It gives you perspective. It keeps you humble. It shows you what you can't always see yourself. And in moments of doubt, it reminds you of your worth.

Whether it's a mentor, a peer, or a trusted friend, the community is where transformation begins. It's where collaboration sparks innovation. And where accountability fuels growth.

The right people will not only celebrate your success but will also provide a supportive space for your challenges.

Because when we grow together, we grow stronger.

The Three Pillars of G.R.I.T.

Every thriving business stands on a foundation of:

1. **Resilience & Adaptability** Entrepreneurship is a rollercoaster. The strongest leaders don't avoid failure—they learn from it. They pivot with grace, bounce back with courage, and use adversity as fuel for their next breakthrough.

2. **Vision & Strategic Thinking** Great entrepreneurs dream beyond the moment. They plan, prepare, and stay aligned with their purpose. They anticipate, adapt, and make decisions with the long game in mind.

3. **Execution & Discipline** Ideas alone aren't enough. Discipline turns dreams into reality. The most successful entrepreneurs show up daily, especially when it's hard. They take consistent action, knowing that small steps compound into big impact.

How to Build the Business and the Life You DESERVE:

- **Discipline**: Set realistic goals. Build habits. Track your progress. Show up—especially when motivation fades. Discipline sustains momentum.

- **Engagement:** Stay visible. Stay curious. Support others. Embrace feedback. Be willing to shift course when needed. Growth requires flexibility.

- **Strategy**: Learn from others. Read. Attend workshops. Ask, "What's my long game?" And map your moves with intention.

- **Execution**: Focus on progress over perfection. Take bold, consistent action. Let momentum carry you forward.

- **Resilience**: Let yourself fail—and grow. Journal, seek coaching, and connect with those who've weathered storms. Reframe challenges as stepping stones.

- **Vision**: Get clear on your "why." Picture where you want to be in 5–10 years, then reverse-engineer your path with confidence and clarity.

- **Empowerment**: Own your voice. Trust your journey. Lift others as you rise. True success is rooted in helping others realize their potential, too.

The journey of entrepreneurship has tested me, stretched me, and refined me. It's also connected me with extraordinary people and led me to my true purpose.

If you're reading this and you've felt discouraged, doubted, or defeated, know this: Your story matters. Your voice is needed. And your path is uniquely yours.

You don't have to do this alone. Whether you join a community like G.R.I.T., find a mentor, or simply start sharing your story—take the step. Growth begins with intention, and greatness follows those who keep showing up.

Together, let's rise with grace. Let's lead with heart. And let's build something that truly lasts.

Jennifer Bardot, MA, MS, is a publisher and author of the Deconstructing GRIT Collection and Owning Your G.R.I.T.—five international bestselling anthologies available at Target, Walmart, Barnes & Noble, and Amazon. She is featured on the cover of *St. Louis Small Business Monthly* as 2021's "Top 100 Persons to Know to Help Grow Your Business," was awarded the President's Circle by Enterprise Bank & Trust, received the Titan 100 honor in 2024, was named one of the 2024 Most Influential Women in Construction by the National Association of Women in Construction (NAWIC), and has been seen on NBC, ABC, CNN, Fox2, and other media platforms.

Founder of the GRIT Community—a free women's leadership group with over one thousand members—Jennifer holds a BA and dual master's degrees, has an active life and health insurance license, holds certificates in the Dare to Lead Training by Brené Brown, and has participated in Women in Leadership and Leadership St. Louis by FOCUS St. Louis. She served as a mentor for Lindenwood University, St. Louis University, Washington University, and Fontbonne University. She was the Leukemia & Lymphoma Society's visionary in 2024.

Jennifer is passionate about supporting business owners and leaders, is a dedicated mother to three boys, and is an outdoor adrenaline adventurer.

Please scan the QR code to connect with this author.

G.R.I.T.

Lisa York

Full Circle to Finding Momentum

My hope is that this chapter will encourage you to know that regardless of your background or any hardships you have encountered, you can be what you want to be and have the success you desire. Your past doesn't determine your future.

I was born in the 60s in San Francisco at the beginning of the hippie era. My upper-middle-class parents had everything: a beautiful home, fancy cars, and jewelry. They weren't happy, so they sold everything, bought a school bus, converted it into living space, and took off with three kids (I am the eldest) and a dog in tow.

We traveled through most states, and they were trying everything to "find" happiness. Yoga, meditation, vegetarianism, and weed. We even lived in a nudist camp. Nothing was fulfilling.

They drove the bus to Mexico. We parked on the beach. I rode horses up and down the beach and went to school there. My mom got typhoid fever, so they came back to the States to get medical treatment, and she recovered.

My parents had friends in Granada. They sold the bus and went to live there. It was lovely, the weather was great, and yet, still, my mom and dad were not fulfilled.

They went to Florida. Money was running out, so they purchased a station wagon and a tent and then drove to Maine. We pitched the tent every night. In Maine, they rented a house, and my dad started a book-keeping business. They had a fourth child, and we lived in a small house.

My mom and dad were born Jewish, so they wanted to go to Israel and join a Kibbutz. My mom found out there was a community much closer, so they should investigate. My mom and dad went to visit it in Connecticut and then joined the community.

The community was Christian and much like the Amish—no phone, no newspaper, and little contact with the outside world. They gave what was left of their worldly possessions and got settled. We lived in an apartment on the grounds, and my mom went to work sewing modest clothes or preparing the communal meals. Many of the meals were inexpensive, like liver. I used to smother it with Ketchup to drown out the taste, and because of that, to this day, I cannot stomach Ketchup.

My dad went to work in the factory helping to build wooden toys for children, which they sold to schools to support themselves. They had a school on the premises, so my siblings and I were in school every day.

There were four community locations: Connecticut, Pennsylvania, New York, and England. They found out my father had flown private planes in California. He and another man started flying between communities. On December 30, 1974, just after my eleventh birthday, my dad and his co-pilot crashed and were both killed. The community didn't believe in birth control. The co-pilot's family had twelve kids. My mom was six weeks pregnant with baby number six.

Many years later, I was happy to learn my dad had finally found peace and happiness when he accepted Jesus Christ as his savior in the community. I also eventually accepted Jesus and am convinced this is the only place to find peace and happiness.

My dad was an only child, and his parents were horrified at what had transpired with their perfect child. Once he was gone, they wanted us to leave the community, but we had a lot of support and didn't want to go.

The community moved us to England. I lived there for six years. We went on field trips, and I saw some sights, but because we were isolated in the community, I didn't know anything about the economy.

The community believed that when you reached high school age, you should go to the local public high school in the town where you were located. This was so you could decide whether to stay or possibly leave the community. I wouldn't have left because they warned us about the dangers of the outside world, like boys, drugs, and rock and roll music. I was terrified.

Another girl and I went to high school dressed in our odd conservative clothing. It was difficult, but at least we had each other. Eventually, the community decided my mom wasn't meeting the requirements of living there. They told her she needed to take some "time away" and think about how to change. The community sent us back to Connecticut and put us in a small house. My mom hadn't seen money, driven a car, or worked in seven years, so she was a little panicked. My grandparents came and moved us closer to them in Massachusetts.

There were seven of us with a couple of bedrooms and one bathroom. It wasn't fun. We never went naked or hungry, but my mom took three jobs, and food stamps were helpful. I grew up fast and helped raise the kids.

After college, I had the opportunity to move to St. Louis, Missouri, for my first job, and I jumped at the chance to get away from all the bratty little kids. I didn't know anyone and had never been to the Midwest, but I was excited about the opportunity. The job was working as a customer service representative, and the plan was to get a territory and go into sales. I quickly realized it was a very chauvinistic field, and all the men got promoted into the field and not the women. I did get a promotion, but I was so young and stupid, I didn't realize I got a title, more work, but no additional money. Lesson learned. Make sure you are earning what you are worth.

Needless to say, I found another job selling advertising for a local newspaper. I was starting with nothing—no leads, no accounts. I was out cold calling all the time. I found success there, but it was easy to lose accounts because the copy people didn't talk to the advertising people and would sometimes write derogatory articles about your clients, and you would lose them. Very frustrating.

After working in St. Louis, Missouri, for a couple of years, I met my amazing husband, Michael. We were married in a beautiful ceremony at the Missouri Botanical Garden and settled into married life in a small but cute apartment. Life was good, and we were happy. We bought a house, got a dog, and were a true American family!

Fortunately, Michael and I ran into a college buddy of his. He worked in promotions for a local top 40 radio station and said they were hiring. I got the job, but had no idea how hard it was going to be. Talk about cold calling. My friend and I started at the same time. At Christmas, there was a tree in the station's foyer. We were encouraged to decorate it. We ripped off the front of the phone book and hung it on there and wrote "our account list" as a joke, but it wasn't really.

I learned persistence and how to deal with a lot of rejection. The station was sold, I became pregnant with our first child, and I was happy to quit to be a stay-at-home mom. Unfortunately, Michael was a victim of layoffs, and nine months later, I had to go back to work. I wanted to get back into the radio business and was fortunate yet again to land a position with the number-one-rated station at the time. This was the peak of radio listening, and although our ad space timeframes were constantly sold out because of the high demand, the challenge was to get a higher dollar for each commercial. Thankfully, it was easier than the last job.

I quit after the third baby. We needed extra money, so I became an independent contractor with a home-based jewelry company. This job change allowed me to be with the kids and make my own schedule. It was the heyday of home parties, so I was doing eight to ten parties a month and sponsoring jewelers. This job was the beginning of my entrepreneurial journey. I was in control of my own time and had to be self-motivated, a very necessary skill needed to own your own business.

Although jewelry is a fun industry, and I was always a walking advertisement, there were still challenges. I had to carry the jewelry cases and set up the displays. Sometimes, there were little kids who would play with the jewelry, and the moms wouldn't stop them! I was working nights. I would print off a map to get to the hostess's home, and I often got lost coming home in the dark.

Hostesses sometimes cancelled at the last minute, which was an aggravation. We would go to the annual conference, and all the ladies went out shopping. I went with them, but could never buy anything because money was still a little tight for us. I was grateful for the opportunity to be home with my kids, of course, so I persevered.

My life was perfect for me. I loved taking care of the kids, driving them to and from school, being room mom, and teaching library and art classes. I knew all their friends, and the house was always filled with their friends. It was a blissful twenty-three years.

Then the kids grew up. What was I going to do? My life's purpose was seemingly gone. My brother owned a merchant services company and offered me a job. I turned it down, saying I had been my own boss for so long that I couldn't work for anyone else. He said it was a 1099 position, and I could still be my own boss. I said I would try it, but didn't think I would like it. What I had forgotten was how much I liked working with local businesses back in my radio days. I loved this job!

The early days working for my brother were some of the most challenging I had ever experienced. I was still in sales, but in a completely new industry that I knew nothing about. This is a very saturated industry with a lot of underhanded people. It basically means that cold calling is extremely difficult because merchants are inundated with people calling on them.

I finally realized it would be a good idea to contact everyone I had ever done business with: my jeweler, vet, furniture store, and auto repair shop. I told them I had started a new gig and asked if I could practice on them. They all said yes, I saved them all money, and they all switched to me.

I realized that maybe I can do this. My first paycheck was only $19, but I didn't let that deter me. I started networking like a crazy person, and the referrals started coming. I was very grateful that the hard work was paying off.

With hard work, determination, and discipline, I built a successful business working for my brother, but soon realized there would be many advantages for me and my clients if I could work for myself instead. Despite the fear, I took a leap of faith and formed an LLC and haven't looked back.

Each day has its own challenges, but you must keep in mind the big picture. I'm so grateful to be my own boss. About a year ago, I received a cancer diagnosis, and I don't know how I would have coped if I had a corporate job.

Throughout our thirty-five years of marriage, there have been many ups and downs. Our three awesome kids are the highlight, of course. Some of the lows were surgeries and job layoffs, and the untimely death of my younger brother.

Looking back, I would never have chosen the crazy life I had. However, it is very clear to me how all my experiences contributed to my current success. The ability to pivot, adjust to different situations, and survive difficulties is so important!

There are so many blessings and opportunities to be found if you just keep your eyes open, take a leap of faith, and work hard. Be determined to thrive in every situation.

Lisa York resided in O'Fallon, Illinois, for thirty-two years. She lived with her amazing husband, Michael, whom she was married to for thirty-five years.

They have three wonderful children: Jessica is a CPA, married to Jeff, and lives in St. Louis, Missouri. Aaron is in the Air Force. He currently lives in England with his wife Chieko. They are about to have Lisa and Michael's first grandchild. Jacob is in logistics, living in New Hampshire with his girlfriend, Janae, but they could end up anywhere as he works remotely.

Lisa was the Alignable O'Fallon Businessperson of the year twice and BNI Belleville All Star twice.

Her personal relationship with Jesus Christ was of the utmost importance to her. She enjoyed playing the violin in her church orchestra. She and Michael loved to travel and participate in fun activities like concerts, plays, the Missouri Botanical Garden, and the zoo.

G.R.I.T.

Jim Adolphson

When the Unthinkable Happens

On January 15, 2021, the text came through at 4:26 p.m., and it read "he has passed." My heart sank, and I remember thinking, *What now?* It was like any other Friday, I was up at 5 a.m., I had exercised, journaled, and had an email exchange with my partner about a wire that was coming in from a sale.

As I arrived at work that morning, something just felt off; someone had attempted to gain access to our bank account. When I called the 800-number for the bank, they told me I needed to get to the nearest branch with my ID as soon as possible. I called my partner on the way, as he lived in another state, but there was no answer. Thankfully, when I arrived at the bank, they let me know that everything was okay—but man, they had my heart racing! It turned out someone in the call center had overreacted and sent me into a panic over a simple security measure.

As I left the bank, I attempted to call my partner again, but there was still no answer. Then my phone rang. It was his spouse on the other end of the line, asking if I had talked to him. She had come home for the weekend to visit family, but hadn't heard from him since the night before. I told her that we had communicated earlier that day and that I was trying to reach him as well.

As I walked in the door that Friday evening, the message came through. I told my wife that he was dead, and she just looked at me in disbelief. I remember that night, my mind raced with questions: *What now? Why? How?* I spent the evening notifying my staff and trying to be the rock they needed as I shared the terrible news. When I awoke Saturday morning, I had a sense of *it's all up to you, Jim.* You have sixteen families depending on you. I started to think about how and when I will notify our clients. What will they say? How will the company be affected? Do I need to replace him? Can I take on his role as well? What in the world just happened?

As we all started arriving at work on Monday morning, we gathered to talk about the future of the company. I assured everyone that we were a strong, resilient group, and as much of a travesty as this was, we were going to survive and make it. The staff reassured me that they were all-in and were there for me as much as I was there for them, but we all knew the work had just begun. The staff went about their normal tasks, and I went into the office and started making the list of all the things that needed to happen. We had to change all the passwords on everything, and that list was longer than you could ever imagine. I had to figure out who I could move into the role as my right-hand person. After all, my partner had just passed away, and I needed someone to help me guide the ship.

The phone calls and emails started as soon as I closed the office door. People had heard of the tragedy over the weekend and wanted to extend their condolences. It was one of the most exhausting days I have had as an entrepreneur. And the tough part was just beginning. One of the first tasks was to pull out the operating agreement and make sure that I had the authority to make all the decisions without jeopardizing anything. This was quickly followed up with a call to my attorney to review the operating agreement and prepare for everything that was going to be coming down the pipeline. Even though you think you are organized, that doesn't prepare you for the password that was reset but not updated on the master list, or for all the two-factor authentications that went to your partner's phone, which you don't have access to because it is in another state.

You don't realize how jammed up you can become when a death certificate is required to remove someone from a bank account, as an authorized user on a credit card, or as the primary user on your Office 365 account. It is easy to become burned out as you must repeat the tragedy over and over again, because the person on the other end of the line has no idea what happened, but still has a policy they must follow. And just when you think things are moving in a direction where you can get back to the new normal, the probate attorney calls and gives you the *"I'm the good guy"* song and dance, but then asks, *"What do you have for the family?"* You then must explain to him that an operating agreement was in place, and the deceased did not sign off on or agree to his life insurance policy, because he thought it was a waste of money.

Having said that, there is still a human factor to all of this. You now have a widow and a son who have lost a husband, a father, and their primary source of income. What, and how, do you make things right for them?

There was never any question about doing the right thing for the family or not, but what was the right thing—who determined what that was? It was time to have a meeting with our silent partner to help determine how to handle things moving forward and decide what was fair. After all, we were just coming out of the pandemic—we were all unsure how things were going to look moving forward, and we were full of questions. Are all our clients going to be in the same situation and able to still provide us the same volume of material as they were before the pandemic? What can we afford to pay out to ensure that we don't jeopardize the safety and financial stability of the business moving forward? Is the probate attorney going to have an opinion? What authority, if any, does he have over our decision?

After going back and forth with the probate attorney and making no meaningful headway, we determined that the widow would retain ownership for ninety days while we figured things out. Not one to let loose ends go, I decided to call her to discuss what would be fair for everyone. The conversation started with her letting me know that she had let the attorney go because she felt he was making things worse and not better. The conversation was positive and productive. As we talked through the details, we agreed on the dollar amount that she was happy with, which would also not hurt the company financially. On another positive note, she was familiar with the company attorney and agreed to him drafting the settlement.

We got together for hopefully the last uncomfortable meeting—uncomfortable in that it was filled with tears because it was a sad day for all of us, knowing it was the end of an era. We made it through that meeting, wished each other the best, agreed to keep in touch, and support each other in any way we could. We have kept in touch over the years and continue to stay connected through social media. The business has moved on, but still has, and always will have, the spirit of the one we lost built into its ideals and principles. When I look back on this time in our journey, there are so many lessons I've learned—things you wish would have been done differently. But it's easy to be the armchair quarterback after the fact.

First and foremost, the advice I would give to any entrepreneur is to make sure that you have an operating agreement in place that is created by an attorney, not one you do online. Any good attorney will know stories like mine and will have a lot of thoughts on how to best structure the operating agreement to protect the members and the company. Key man insurance is also a must. Just like anything, it comes with a cost, and you might not ever use it, but in my case, I sure wish I had had it. Make sure you have a plan in place to update your passwords regularly, and if there is a two-factor authentication in place, that the access is easily accessible to you and your partner. Think about duplicating yourself or cross-training someone to be able to do your job, just in case you face a situation similar to the one I experienced. The business needs to survive without you. It is, after all, part of the legacy that all of us entrepreneurs hope to leave behind.

At the end of the day, lead with your heart; good things happen to good people, even in times of tragedy. The business survived and is prospering. The family has grown and is moving forward without forgetting, and the dream of someone who has passed lives on through others.

Jim is the CEO of Adonis Holdings, where he has successfully led an R2v3-certified recycling center for over a decade. Adonis Holdings offers comprehensive IT asset recovery solutions tailored to businesses of all sizes, specializing in data destruction services that are verified by third-party audits.

A graduate of Missouri State University with a Bachelor of Science in Hospitality Administration and Business Management, Jim combines his business expertise with a commitment to philanthropy, donating over a million dollars in equipment, time, and resources over the past twelve years.

Deeply passionate about conservation, Jim spends much of his time working on his farm and enjoying the outdoors through hunting and fishing. A devoted husband to Jenny and proud father to his son Kalob, Jim is currently writing a children's book about e-waste recycling to inspire the next generation of environmental stewards.

Please scan the QR code to connect with this author.

G.R.I.T.®

Gary Baker

The Pursuit of Fulfillment

If anyone really knows me, they know that as soon as I start understanding something, I immediately break it down to get to the essence or source and then create a visual image of my understanding. Therefore, in contemplating this chapter, I thought: What is the essence of G.R.I.T? Where does it come from? Why is it needed? Why are Growth, Resilience, Intention, and Tenacity part of being an entrepreneur?

The definition of grit is:

1. small loose particles of stone or sand indicating the grade of fineness of an abrasive

2. courage and resolve; strength of character

Let's have some fun and tackle grit with the first definition. Grit is small or loose particles that are produced by something being grinded. But where does it come from? How many times have we heard as entrepreneurs, we have to grind? Far too many, but it is the truth.

GRIND = G.R.I.T.

Growth: The first letter of G.R.I.T. comes from grinding it out. The benefit of the grind is the grit particles that are produced to become what you need to be an entrepreneur. The particles produced from the grind fall into the categories of resilience, intention, and tenacity.

For me, growth has two parts: a beginning and an end, which we will tackle later. For the beginning, growth starts with a relentless curiosity and a love for learning. This involves constantly asking questions and striving for self-improvement—to become more, to understand more, and to do more. Taking the step towards growth takes courage, and once you take that step, life starts to happen. The "growth" you imagined never happens how you expect and want it to. The beginning stages of growth are what form the foundation for the other elements of G.R.I.T.—the resilience, intention, and tenacity.

Let's get personal for a minute: Where do you get your grit from? Take a minute to think back over your life and the adversities you have faced. Your understanding of where your grit came from is a gift—a gift that is waiting for you to find and use to grow in all aspects of life.

For me, the grind of life started early. My parents had me when they were eighteen and nineteen years old. My dad owned two bars—the legal drinking age was only twenty-one in 1976. Being raised by young parents who owned two bars was a chaotic, unpredictable, and uncertain life. So, what does one do when life is chaotic, unpredictable, and uncertain? Most run from it or ignore it. But the courageous ones fight through it.

However, as children, we often don't know we have choices. We just think, "This is life. This is how the world works." So, I started to navigate the world—living my life, hanging out with friends, playing sports, and going to school—just as everyone else did. I did normal things, but I also had added stresses in life that most didn't. It was just my normal life, and I started getting good at living with uncertainty, learning quickly how to navigate life through chaos.

One thing that is very clear throughout my story is that despite all the chaos in my life, I never doubted my parents' love for me. I reflect on that often. I know that, regardless of circumstance or environment, being loved, supported, and encouraged is all someone needs to get through the tough times.

As I entered my twenties, I learned how different my childhood was compared to my peers. I realized that I had something most people didn't have at a very young age: I had resilience. I created a level of ambition, desire, fortitude, confidence, and courage that most didn't have. I saw what I had overcome in life and how it was becoming a skillset instead of a drawback. I decided that I would live my life by who I wanted to be and who I would help, not by my circumstance, my environment, or other people's opinions of me.

Resilience: The ability to bounce back from adversity. Navigating a chaotic life as a child forged an early foundation of resilience—one that would become my "Teflon" armor.

Let's move to **intention**; after living through chaos, surviving and thriving from it, I discovered I wanted to help others navigate the pathway from uncertainty to possibility. Because I knew it could be done, I wanted to help others do the same. I thought I would go into psychology, but after a long conversation with my grandfather, he shared that I could still help people through business. I went to his house on weekends as my place of refuge, often. We did the same thing every weekend—I would do some project for him, and he would pay me for doing it. He believed that work came first, and then we grilled something on the back porch and talked about "life, liberty and the pursuit of happiness." He believed anything was possible with the right mindset, heart, and desire. He had a curiosity and love for what is possible that I could feel in every conversation. The next morning, he made eggs, and we read the business section as we talked about companies and stock prices. I loved those conversations.

One day, his financial advisor called him. He passed the phone to me and said, "Maybe you would want to do what Jim does since you like business and stocks." So, I asked Jim what he did on a daily basis, and what he said sealed the deal for me: "Gary, I know you like stocks and the markets, but I deal with people, not just with money. Half the time, I feel like I am a psychologist versus a money manager." Right then and there, I knew I would become a financial advisor. People and investing—that was my dream job.

So that's what I did. I earned my MBA in Personal Finance and started my career as a financial advisor to help people. But what I didn't fully appreciate when I started was that my desire to help people would ultimately drive my career and create the business model we have today.

Intention: Having a clear sense of purpose. For me, this manifested into a laser focus on helping others, solving problems, and providing solutions for what is most important to them in life. Every year, my goal is to become better personally and professionally so I can do more of the work I love to do for others. Our company continues to do this in ways I never could have imagined when I had that conversation with my grandfather's advisor in 1994. Which brings me back to the final aspect of G.R.I.T.

Tenacity: The unwavering persistence to stick with a goal; to move forward despite obstacles. This is the inner voice that refuses to accept defeat. I don't think I have ever lost at anything—which is completely untrue, but also isn't untrue when you don't quit. I had to pivot. I had huge setbacks, and I made dumb mistakes and decisions. But I have never once quit on my vision and purpose of helping people understand who they are, why they exist, and where they can best express their gifts and talents to leave a lasting impact on the world for generations to come. With a purpose like that, why would I ever quit?

Your purpose is rooted in your passion-filled desire to serve the people who can benefit the greatest from your insights, experiences, education, and guidance. Once you have your purpose, tenacity becomes the force that helps you endure and overcome all the challenges you'll face. G.R.I.T. is only the starting point for growth; it's the second part of growth that truly matters. Life is about who you become, what you do, who you serve, and how you help people in life. The spirit of growth should be rooted in a passion-filled purpose and driven by what is most important to you, which is represented in your core values and in the principles that guide your decisions. Once you have the foundations of G.R.I.T. and a sense of purpose that is driven by what's most important to you, the true journey in life begins: the pursuit of success and fulfillment.

Think about the following questions:

- What does success mean to you?

- What does fulfillment mean to you?

- Are they the same, or are they different?

- What are you chasing—success, fulfillment, or both?

Success is often measured by *external* markers like wealth, status, and achievements—everything outside of us that others can see. Our confidence is created here, in validation, admiration, and acknowledgement.

Fulfillment is an *internal* state of deep satisfaction and peace. Fulfillment is the true joy that comes from purpose-driven endeavors. The elusive nature of fulfillment can be monitored through our commitment to our purpose, which stems from a deep understanding of self; it is where our courage comes from. Note the differences between confidence and courage—both are needed, but they are different. I get to live my dream of being part psychologist and part investor. Everything I do in life is in some way, shape, or form a combination of the two.

I would never have been able to do all I have done if I hadn't experienced everything earlier in life. What some may consider a difficult way to grow up, I see as my greatest training ground for grit. Yes, times were challenging, to say the least. But the love of my parents, grandparents, my wife, my kids, my friends, and mentors has made it all possible and fulfilling.

My wife has been the most instrumental person in my life and has helped me become who I am today. She has ten times the level of grit I have, because she has had to use all of it to just deal with me and all my visions, thoughts, ideas, and whiteboards. My point in bringing this up is that I believe choosing your spouse is the most important decision you can make in life, other than your commitment to your faith. I know that the fulfillment I desire in life will be found in what we do together for the rest of our lives, rooted in the faith we share.

My advice, made simple, is this:

Take real adventure in life. Seek who you are from the inside out—and see what you discover through the grind of all you've been through in life. I bet you will find deposits of grit that you never knew existed—sources of grit that will ignite the passion of your spirit.

Find your passion-filled purpose. You will find that purpose in overcoming the adversities of life. Combine that purpose with your God-given gifts and talents, and you will live a life like you never imagined. Your purpose can be found in guiding others who are afraid to take the path you have already conquered, or in sharing the wisdom of your experiences with those who may need it to live the life they imagine.

Don't get lost. When you have a surplus supply of grit, are inspired with purpose, and led by what is most important to you, you are on your way toward success and fulfillment. Pay close attention, though, because this is where we can get lost quickly. Success and fulfillment can be different, but they can also be the same. Imagine two circles: one is success, the other fulfillment. The overlap in the center is purpose. If lived properly, they start to overlap each other and grow toward each other. As they do, the overlap in the center, where purpose lives, grows bigger.

My goal in life is to become *successful* at being *fulfilled*—that's what I work toward every day. Our business model is based on that! I couldn't do what I do, nor would I want to, without everyone on the team. They are the best people to work with in making the vision we have a reality!

As managing partner of Undivided Wealth Management and the founder of Relational Advisor Organization and Evolation Consulting, Gary has developed a unique relational approach that focuses on what truly matters most to his clients.

Gary has been recognized as one of the *Fastest Growing Advisors to Watch* by Advisor Hub. He has served on the Kestra Private Wealth Council and the Fidelity Advisor Council. Undivided Wealth Management has received the Humanitarian Service Award, the Partnership and Culture Award, and the Most Innovative Firm.

Gary most recently joined the board of FSI Institute. He serves as an adjunct professor at Washington University and mentors MBA students at Saint Louis University. Gary holds a B.A. in finance from the University of Missouri–Columbia and an MBA from Washington University.

Gary is led by his faith and is a devoted husband to Sarah and father of three children, Jack, Charlie, and Abbey.

Please scan the QR code to connect with this author.

G.R.I.T.

Sarah Bravo

Bravo...Sarah Bravo!

It was the summer of 1993, the year that two very significant things happened in my life that would change the trajectory of my future forever. I was 17 going on 18, graduating from high school with a five-month-old baby boy. Clearly on a track that wasn't expected or planned. College wasn't going to be an option. In fact, from my perspective, I was on track to becoming another statistic: a teenage single mom who'd probably end up on government assistance, at best, living paycheck to paycheck, struggling to make ends meet...probably beginning a cycle that my son would be destined to duplicate. Finding myself with this huge responsibility, I was overwhelmed, confused, but mostly, just a young, scared teenage girl, trying to now take care of a baby. I had no idea what I was going to do. Fortunately, rather than seeing my future as burdened, I looked at my son and immediately got inspired. I got motivated. While I had been lost before, unsure what I would do with my life, I now wanted to succeed. Succeed at what? Well, that was the question.

Having my son was the spark that catapulted me into action. I quickly found a job in order to start making an income. This wasn't the permanent job; it was the "just get by" position while I figured out what my 18-year-old self was going to do. In my spare time, I scoured the newspaper looking for something that would provide enough money to get by.

But not just "provide." I wanted more, I wanted all the things that I saw other people have. I grew up in Los Angeles, California, so the idea of the "Hollywood dream" was a real thing for me. Not the notoriety part, but the financial security part about making enough money that I could do what I wanted to, when I wanted to do it.

I didn't realize it at the time, but I apparently had an entrepreneurial itch before I even understood what the term meant. Back in the 90s, no one talked a lot about being an entrepreneur; it was looked down upon or classified as something no one ever really made a true living doing. I grew up in an environment where it was preached that to be successful, you have to go to college, get a degree in business, finance, or tech, or something along those lines. All those options seemed like very long and far-off career paths that I knew would not make me happy, but more importantly, put me in the position to pay the bills, like, now.

I heard about an opportunity for a "manager trainee" position. I wasn't exactly sure what this meant or would entail, but when they said I could run my own business, and they'd train and make the initial financial investment in me, I was in. Once they said that the sky's the limit, that I would be my own boss, and that my income would be based on how hard I worked, I knew this was for me. I do also remember my mom saying, "How are you going to manage anyone else? You can't even manage yourself." I didn't know it then, but it was those words, along with the role of being a new mom, that gave me the courage, strength, and motivation to jump into what became a 32-year career path—some might even say, a lifestyle.

I jumped into the wonderful world of entrepreneurship, eyes wide shut. I saw things through rose colored lenses at first. I was ready to jump straight to the top. Then reality kicked in. When I excitedly told people I was going to run my own business and I was in training, many told me this was never going to work, or I was too young, I didn't have any experience, this was a waste of time—anything and everything you could think of that should have made me run away and give up on my dream.

Instead, I used this as fuel to keep me motivated. I used all the negative feedback as encouragement. I could not wait to prove them wrong. I wanted to show them all, "Yes, I can." I read a lot of motivational books, I listened to motivational speakers, and my mentor encouraged me to have confidence in myself, even if no one else did.

He pointed out and asked me to *"Look around, notice all the people that are doing the things that you want to do. If they can, YOU CAN! Someone is going to run their own business, why not you? Someone is going to drive the new car you want, why not you? Someone is going to take the trip that you want to go on, why not you?"* Those words stuck with me, and I said them to myself over and over again, anytime I got discouraged. "It's going to be someone, why not me?"

It wasn't easy for the first several years; it was long hours, long weeks. I can remember working seven days a week, sometimes twelve to thirteen hours a day. I had a plan, I had a goal, and I had a reason. While others were out having fun, spending their weekends at backyard BBQs or social gatherings, just hanging out, I was working and putting all my time, effort, and energy into my business.

I was an independent distributor, tackling direct sales, business-to-business, walking in trying to get someone to buy my product, hearing "no" at least 90-100 times a day, being demeaned and told to "get a real job." On occasion, I would be asked to fill out an application, so that I didn't "have" to do something so embarrassing. Sometimes, I even landed in a parking lot outside of retail shops, talking to strangers, just to get one more sale on the books for the day. I didn't care who I had to talk to, how many people I had to see, or how many times I was rejected. I was on a mission to learn the art of sales and master this skillset, so that

I could open up my own office, hire my own sales team, and be able to duplicate myself.

I was taught one of the most valuable lessons during my training, which I have applied throughout the rest of my career and still apply to this day. As an individual, no matter how good I am or how many sales I make, I am only one person and will eventually hit a ceiling. If I could master this skill, learn to seek out and find others like me, who have a burning desire to succeed, I could teach and train them how to do what I was able to do. Then, that's when I could reach a much greater level of success. As an individual, I'm limited, but as a team, my success is limitless.

The biggest lesson in this, which to me is the best part of being an entrepreneur, is that in order for me to be really successful, I need to teach others how to be successful. I can only grow and reach my goals if I help others that I oversee reach their goals. I learned very early on as an entrepreneur that the more you want to see others succeed, almost by default, you can't help but succeed yourself. Once I mastered the sales part, I opened up my own business. Then I began helping others open their own businesses by teaching and training them what I learned.

After 16 years in direct sales, I trained hundreds of independent contractors on how to sell and how to duplicate themselves. In my company, we were able to take a $20 product and have over one million dollars in sales volume in one year. That was a huge accomplishment, but it is one I could have never reached on my own. It took me learning how to do something, mastering it, and teaching and training others how to do it. It was then that I reached heights well beyond what I had initially set for myself.

It isn't just about sales, production, or even the money. Those are definitely key motivators. But when you find yourself doing well and being able to help others climb the ladder, that, to me, is the real advantage of being an entrepreneur and where the real success lies.

In 2009, I transitioned into a new field, and now, another 16 years later, I have been able to run a very successful residential real estate team in St. Louis, Missouri. All of the lessons I learned early on, the ups and the downs, the easy days and the hard ones, all came into play when I jumped into my new career. This time, however, I jumped in with my eyes wide open.

Today, I still apply the same formula that I used in my previous profession, which took me from salesperson to successful leader, helping hundreds of people become successful entrepreneurs themselves.

I encourage my team members to set goals. I motivate them by pointing out others in our industry who are at the level that they want to be at, and remind them that if that person can do it, so can they. I also share with them how much I want to see them grow. I want to see those on my team surpass every accomplishment, sales record, commission check payout, and more that I have achieved. I encourage this regularly, because once again, in order for me to be successful, I need them to be successful. I can only reach my goals if they reach theirs.

Fast forward. It has now been 32 years since the young, single, teenage mom walked into the wonderful world of entrepreneurship, unsure of herself, and how things would work out. I can confidently say, if I had to start over, I would do it the same, all over again. I have been able to travel the world and take those vacations I once dreamed of, including taking my mom on vacation. By the way, now my mom tells everyone she knows how proud of me she is and how I get my strong work ethic from her. For me, though, the most important part of it all is that not only did I prove the naysayers wrong, but I was able to provide my son with all the things I had hoped I would be able to, including sending him to college and making sure he would graduate debt-free. Most people have to work for a living. Many work very hard for a company, big or small. But if you have to work and are going to work hard, why not do it for yourself?

The road wasn't always easy. There were many times I wanted to give up and just quit. I had a lot of self-doubt at times. I can remember crying in my car because I was just so tired. I would think to myself, "Who am I kidding? I shouldn't have these big dreams." Then I'd remember my "why." I'd refocus on my goals and I'd shake off the negativity, get my attitude right, and bounce back. Having my son reminded me not only why I should have dreams, but I might as well make them big. If it's going to be somebody reaching those big dreams, why not me?

Why not YOU?

Sarah Bravo is proof that hustle, heart, and grit can take you from teen mom to successful entrepreneur. With no formal business degree but a persistent drive to create a better life, she carved a path from being a direct sales rookie to being one of the top leaders in her field.

With over 30 years of experience, Sarah has led teams, mentored like-minded individuals, and now runs one of the top-producing real estate teams in St. Louis, Missouri.

When she's not closing deals or coaching her team, you'll find Sarah traveling to new places, hosting dinner parties for friends, or spending quality time with her son. She's also always up for an adventure—whether it's paragliding off a cliff, ballroom dancing, or horseback riding. Sarah brings positivity, enthusiasm, and an upbeat spirit to everything she does.

Please scan the QR code to connect with this author.

G.R.I.T.

Bing Dempewolf

The Unbreakable Dream

The first time I tried to end my life, I was only eleven years old. I remember being alone in my room, deciding I wanted to end it all, the bitter taste of stolen pills that still lingered on my tongue, and the crushing weight of believing that there was no place for me in this world. But the pain didn't come from the pills themselves—it came from the deep-rooted feeling that I didn't belong anywhere.

My father didn't want a daughter, especially not one born on American soil. From the start, I didn't fit the mold of the obedient, quiet girl he thought a traditional Chinese daughter should be. I was too outspoken. Too curious. Too "American," as he liked to say—like that alone was a dirty word.

At home, it was like walking a tightrope between two worlds. Outside, I was in America, trying to make friends, figure out who I was, and blend in at school. But inside our house, it was all tradition, discipline, and silence. My father didn't care what the world outside looked like—he ruled our home with fear. Every step I took that didn't align with his expectations felt like a threat to him, and he met that with violence. His violence came in the form of hot wheel tracks stacked together or hockey sticks swung at me. He said I was rebellious. I was just trying to survive.

The house was quiet—the kind that feels heavy, like the air itself is pressing down on you. My father's anger still echoed in the walls, his words still sharp in my mind. *You're nothing. You'll never be anything.*

I remember the cold tile of the bathroom floor, the rattle of the medicine cabinet as I opened it. My hands shook as I grabbed the pills—too many of them—and swallowed them one by one, each one a silent scream. *I don't want to be here anymore.* The bitterness coated my tongue, but the real pain wasn't physical. It was the suffocating certainty that I didn't belong—not in my family, not in this world. I was a mistake. A disappointment. And if I disappeared, maybe no one would even notice.

But my body fought back. A friend found me at my house hours later. I was dizzy and sick, my stomach revolting against the poison I'd forced into it. I was taken to the hospital to have my stomach pumped. I curled up in the hospital bed, trembling, wondering why even death seemed to reject me.

I thought that my first suicide attempt would be the last. But pain has a way of festering, of growing roots so deep that sometimes, the only way to survive is to try to destroy yourself before the world can do it for you.

The second time was several months after the first suicide attempt. The despair had sharpened, turned into something relentless. This time, I didn't hesitate. I just took the pills without really thinking about anything else. I don't remember much after the darkness swallowed me. Only flashes—the blur of hospital lights, the frantic voices of doctors, the cold press of an oxygen mask. And then—nothing. I flatlined. My heart stopped. For a few terrifying seconds, I was gone.

But the medical staff refused to let me stay that way. They shocked me back, forced air into my lungs, pulled me from the edge with hands that wouldn't let me fall. When I woke up, there was no relief. Only the crushing weight of being alive when I had wanted so badly not to be.

My mother worked as a nurse on the second floor of the same hospital where I lay in the Emergency Room (ER). The nurse ran upstairs to tell my mom that I was in the ER and that I flatlined but was brought back to life.

After my suicide attempts that year, my father made his final decision: I didn't need to live in our home anymore. I couldn't understand why my dad would kick me out of our home. Who kicks an eleven-year-old out of their home? His reason? I was a girl. A mistake. A burden. And in his eyes, I was born into an Asian family that came to America hoping for a better life—but I wasn't the kind of "new beginning" they had in mind.

What kind of child survives that? The kind who refuses to let her story end in silence. The kind who turns wounds into wisdom. The kind who, at the age of forty-eight, stands at the helm of her own successful Human Resources consulting firm—TAI-CHI Consulting.

Before I knew what the word "resilience" meant, I was living it. At fifteen, my father arranged a marriage for me. No questions, no choices—just tradition and an expectation. Soon after, I became a mother. By twenty-two, I had four children—and a divorce. Friends, relatives, even strangers whispered behind my back, some to my face, that I had ruined my life. They assumed that a young woman with four kids and no husband had nothing left to offer the world.

But deep down, I didn't believe them, I just couldn't. Something inside of me, one could say a stubborn part of me, refused to let go of hope. I believed in one thing with all my heart: *Education would be my salvation! If I couldn't change the past, I could at least shape my future life with education.*

During those chaotic, exhausting, and emotionally draining years of early motherhood, I made a promise to myself—I would get my education, no matter how long it took, no matter how many sleepless nights I faced.

After being kicked out, I didn't know where to go. My mom stepped in as best as she could, but was living under the Asian male influence of how men were often a few strides ahead of the woman, not side by side. Eventually, I ended up at an alternative school—a place for kids who didn't fit anywhere else.

That's where I met Mr. Beil. Unlike the other teachers, he didn't look at me and see a problem; he saw potential. One day after class, he pulled me aside and said, *"You're smarter than you think and stronger than you know."*

I completed my high school diploma, one class at a time, while juggling diapers, dinner, and sometimes two or three jobs just to keep the lights on. Then, I pushed forward to earn multiple college degrees. Each certificate, each class, felt like reclaiming a piece of the life I was once told I couldn't have. I just had grit. My kids saw me struggle, yes, but they also saw me persist. They learned from my actions that giving up was never an option.

Work became my escape, my proving ground, and eventually, my sanctuary. I took whatever job I could get—entry-level, part-time, grave-yard shifts, you name it. I was the call center rep, the assistant who stayed late and showed up early. I observed everything. I asked questions. I kept learning. My work ethic and willingness to do what others wouldn't became my calling card.

Over time, I discovered a natural ability to understand people—not just their needs as employees, but their struggles and dreams. Human Resources wasn't just a job to me; it was a purpose. I didn't just want to fill roles or manage performance reviews. I wanted to build workplaces where people felt seen, heard, and valued— something I had longed for but never found as a child.

For thirty years, I climbed the corporate ladder, moving from admin-istrative roles all the way to the "C" Suite in Human Resources. I worked for organizations across industries and helped shape their HR departments from the ground up. I mentored teams, rebuilt broken systems, and advocated for inclusive, people-centered practices long before it was trendy.

But it wasn't always easy. I walked into rooms where I was the only woman. The only executive with a background full of trauma instead of Ivy League degrees. I faced microaggressions, blatant discrimination, and the quiet burden of never feeling completely "at home" in the spaces I worked so hard to enter. Still, I pushed forward. I built trust through action. I earned respect by showing up prepared, over-delivering, and leading with heart. I turned every challenge into fuel.

Still, something inside me kept whispering: *You were meant for more.* I didn't want to just work for companies—I wanted to create one. I wanted to build something that reflected my values, my story, and my deep belief in the power of people.

And so, TAI-CHI Consulting was born. It wasn't easy. In fact, it felt like everything was stacked against me. As a woman, a survivor of abuse, and someone with no financial safety net, I had to bootstrap everything. There were nights I cried from exhaustion, days when self-doubt crept in, and moments when I felt like I was trying to climb a mountain and was never going to reach the top. I knew how to work with nothing. And more than anything, I knew that I was *ready.*

TAI-CHI Consulting is more than a business. It's a vision realized after decades of fighting to be heard, seen, and respected. We specialize in Human Resources strategies, outsourced HR services, leadership development, and culture building. But our mission goes beyond deliverables. I built this company to be a safe space for organizations to learn how to treat their people better, because no one should feel invisible at work the way I once felt invisible at home.

TAI-CHI stands for balance and harmony. It reflects my belief that business can be both strategic and meaningful. That you can lead with strength and compassion. That honoring people is not only ethical—it's profitable.

There were sacrifices. There were former colleagues who doubted me and family members who questioned my sanity. But I kept going. Because every "no" reminded me that I wasn't building this for them—I was building it for every woman like me who never got a fair shot.

People often ask me how I did it—how I made it from homeless teenager to CEO. The truth is there's no easy answer. There's no secret formula. I survived by doing the next right thing, over and over again. I survived by betting on myself when no one else would. I survived by refusing to let my past define my future.

Entrepreneurship is not for the faint of heart. It requires vision, yes; I had to unlearn a lot of what I was taught growing up. I had to learn that I was worthy of success. That my voice mattered. That my past didn't disqualify me—it *qualified* me in ways others couldn't understand.

Now, when I walk into a boardroom or lead a workshop, I do so with pride. Not because I have a fancy title or a company name on the door, but because I know what it took to get there. I carry my story with me—not as baggage, but as a banner.

I often think back to that eleven-year-old girl, the one who thought the world didn't want her. I wish I could go back and hold her hand, whisper in her ear: *One day, you'll change lives. One day, you'll run your own company. One day, you'll take all this pain and build something powerful from it.*

My story is not one of tragedy. It is one of triumph. It is proof that pain can be turned into purpose, and that even the most broken beginnings can lead to beautiful endings. And to anyone reading this who feels like they don't belong, like they've made too many mistakes, or like it's too late to chase their dreams—I want you to hear me clearly. *You* are *not* broken. *You* are just getting started.

Bing Dempewolf is the founder and CEO of TAI-CHI Consulting, a firm specializing in human resources strategy and culture transformation. With more than three decades of leadership experience, she is known for her trauma-informed, people-first approach to building inclusive, resilient workplace environments.

In addition to her consulting work, Bing serves as the Chief Operating Officer at Mental Health Code, where she contributes to operational leadership in support of mental health, education, and community well-being. She also serves on the board of the St. Louis Society for the Blind and Visually Impaired, advocating for equitable access and essential services.

Outside of her professional roles, Bing is a devoted family member and passionate advocate for dementia and Alzheimer's awareness. Inspired by her personal caregiving journey, her debut book, *Love, Care & Alzheimer's: A Daughter's Memoir*, offers comfort, insight, and support to families navigating memory loss with compassion and courage.

Please scan the QR code to connect with this author.

G.R.I.T.®

Shaun Duvall

Strength Through Surrender

I was the stereotypical gym guy: sitting on a piece of equipment, music blaring in my ears, beads of sweat on my forehead. But then, without warning, the song changed. I didn't anticipate what would happen next...

"Lord, you got me where you want me right now... I wonder what would happen if you could just take this moment, close your eyes, open your hands, surrender, and say, 'Whatever's left, Lord, you can have it.'"

Suddenly, my hands started to open and rise, and tears started sliding down my face in the middle of a packed gym. I had spent years grinding as if it were a badge of honor. That's what grit is supposed to be, right? But at that moment, I wasn't strong. I wasn't winning. I was finally breaking. But what I didn't know was that I was right where I needed to be.

Everybody faces challenges in life: one I didn't fully understand for most of my life was how consistently I struggled with severe ADHD. It wasn't until a year after starting my company, duvari, when I became aware that I wasn't neurotypical. I mean, in my mind, who is really "typical?" Everyone is built differently, each shaped by their past experiences.

Throughout my life, I never fully realized how much ADHD had shaped my need for disciplined systems and the amount of additional work and effort it took to accomplish tasks that seemed to come more easily to my peers. Being an honor student looked different for someone who couldn't just cram the night before. It's interesting that what's categorized on paper as a disability has grown into one of my biggest strengths. Looking back, I couldn't have managed an accelerated MBA, raised a two-year-old, endured a 180-mile round-trip commute for night classes, worked a 50 to 60-hour workweek, settled into a new city, and led a new team without the systems that came as a by-product of being neurodivergent. They weren't a choice, but a necessity.

However, that same strength that I unknowingly relied on also left me most vulnerable to upcoming events I wouldn't have ever imagined, especially in such a short period. I thought I could take on whatever life threw at me. This badge of honor was a facade. It placed me in a hospital on multiple occasions with chest pains and more wires hanging from my body than I like to admit. Were the internal warning lights going off? No, that would have been too logical. I kept doing what had always worked up to that point: I just kept pushing forward. That was until I finally found myself as that weirdo in the gym, with tears in my eyes and hands raised, realizing I had nothing left.

So, what led up to this point? It started with the unraveling of a seventeen-year marriage. That marked the beginning of a two-year divorce process and a complete shift in family dynamics. Everything that once felt familiar was suddenly different, from always finding my identity in being able to do daily life with my kids to having a quiet shell of a home and an empty feeling.

At the same time, my future business partner informed me that he would no longer partner with the company we were set to build. What was even harder for me was that he was more than just a business partner to me: he was the friend who had given me the courage to take the leap as an entrepreneur. It was now just months before the company's launch, and the one employee I was hiring and training called unexpectedly. She shared that her plans had changed, and she was moving out of state to be closer to her sister, who was facing a serious health issue. I completely understood, but I just sat there thinking, "*What just happened?*" Nothing about starting the company was unfolding the way I thought—not even close!

I began to second-guess my decision to quit the thriving job I had previously held. Building a company on my own started feeling more like building a plane *while* flying it, seeing smoke occasionally, only to realize the flames are coming from every direction, thinking, "*When is this going to end?*" That's what it felt like to lose any semblance of what once brought me comfort. Everything around me was new. I was in a different house, only able to see my children half the time. An eerie, unwanted silence filled the house, reminding me of what I had once considered home base—my children. When business finally began to gain traction, add team members, and eventually a partner who shared the same vision, life handed me another unexpected blow.

One Saturday evening, I was a passenger with two friends in a serious ATV accident: it was a moment where God's presence was undeniable. Riding at nearly full speed with two close friends, we suddenly saw a sunken area where the land had settled. We tried to maneuver around it but instead hit a tree stump head-on, launching the side-by-side into a series of flips. I was ejected midair, thrown through the windshield, and landed several feet away.

I was rushed to the emergency trauma center with extensive facial and head injuries: nearly scalped with my face deeply cut. And yet, a day later, I was filled with the oddest sense of gratitude. Literally, some people close to me thought I must have really hit my head too hard! I never questioned whether I would show up for our team huddle that Monday, just a day and a half later. I always believe in controlling what you can control. If I am breathing, I am showing up. That morning, I logged in online to lead the huddle. But looking back, I see now that by pushing through as I had always done, I missed something important: I was surrounded by people who truly cared and wanted to support me, but I did not allow them to care for me at the level I should have. I took away their opportunity to give, to care, to be part of my healing process. Letting people in is not a sign of weakness. That moment was another reminder of how quickly everything can change and how important it is to surround yourself with the right people. Not just to be strong for them, but to let them be strong for you. I believe we were placed here to serve, and when I allow others to lift me up, it not only strengthens me, it also fills them.

Going through this series of trials in such a short period of time—building a company, navigating a divorce, losing a business partner, experiencing the loss of my first employee before they even started, and healing from a life-changing accident—I discovered what truly mattered. I learned that my prayers are rarely answered by taking the pain away. They are answered through opportunities to build character through perseverance. This is why Romans 5:3-5 will always hold substantial meaning for me: because of the promise that "...we glory in our sufferings, because we know that suffering produces perseverance; perseverance, character; and character, hope, which comes from the Holy Spirit" (NIV). This is why we should take heart: because when suffering occurs, that is when God can do His best work. We aren't always rescued by the fire, but if you choose to surrender to the God who is power, you will be strengthened and refined by it.

The one question I get asked most frequently is, "What led you to start your own company?" It all started with an intentional pause, which, for me, doesn't come naturally. I took a few months to reflect, working through a workbook that, at the time, was intended to prepare me for a promotion with my previous company. Instead of preparing me for that future leadership role, it completely changed my path.

What I once thought I wanted quickly became less important, as I experienced a mental shift that came from discovering what meant the most to me. It's amazing how I have always found myself chasing what felt important in those moments, believing it would bring me happiness, only to still feel a sense of emptiness. It is amazing how much additional energy can come from having a clear purpose. It wasn't a self-centered purpose, but rather the fulfillment I receive from helping someone recognize their own potential through their unique gifts—moving them closer to their purpose.

When I set out to create my company, duvari, it was never just about the staffing or monetary rewards of building a business. It was about creating something with a real purpose. After having experienced these trials—the loss and uncertainty—I realized that I could not carry it all on my own. Just as the lyrics to the song "Surrender" by Rob Hardin of Rare of Breed express, true strength is not something I can consistently manufacture. It only comes when I let go and surrender.

Surrendering doesn't come easily for me, and it did not take away all the pain. What it did do was give me the peace and hope I needed in the middle of it. It opened the door for others to breathe life into me. It taught me the importance of allowing people to support me and allowing myself to be vulnerable with others, even if some relationships are only for a season.

Through these unexpected turns, I have gained deeper self-awareness and a greater sense of empathy. I've been given the blessing of a blended family with multiple children who are navigating high levels of ADHD and autism. As a result, I now see people differently. I see—and can better approach—those who are going through family struggles and wrestling with depression and anxiety, because I have now felt what that is like. I can now genuinely relate to those who have questioned the point of living. I've come to see that the trials in life have given me gifts that I couldn't have gained any other way.

This journey has equipped me to help others uncover their own purpose, use their unique gifts, and help them find strength through their own surrender. That is my calling. This is what duvari was built for—to develop holistic people who lead with love, seek clarity, serve with intention, and leave a positive, lasting impact.

One of the most full-circle and fulfilling moments of my journey as a business owner came from an early act of belief. Before duvari was built, my original partner, who couldn't continue with me, still honored his commitment to financially support me during that critical year leading up to the launch. Years later, I ran into him and shared that, thanks to his investment and belief in me, we were able to pay it forward by writing a check for the same substantial amount to a startup company. This support helped them launch their mission to foster self-awareness in others, align with their true fulfillment, and lead a life of purpose.

Now, being able to lead a company focused on truly impacting lives, I have the opportunity to create initiatives that reflect our core values, such as sponsoring one child around the world per team member, so that we can instill the principle of serving others first. What once looked like struggles have become tools I now use to lead by example, help others see their value, understand their unique gifts and purpose, and know that they matter. None of this could have happened until I learned that real strength comes only through surrender. Because this fight was never mine to carry alone.

Shaun Duvall is the founder and managing partner of duvari, a St. Louis–based IT staffing company with a people-first mission. In a world of transactional business models, Shaun set out to build something different—an organization focused on holistic team development through its High-Performance Hearts philosophy.

Shaun believes the future belongs to those who lead with heart, listen with intention, and act with purpose. Duvari has become a trusted partner to clients ranging from startups to global enterprises, all while staying grounded in its core principle of bringing fulfillment through clarity. Outside of work, Shaun is devoted to his family and passionate about mentoring the next generation of purpose-driven leaders.

Please scan the QR code to connect with this author.

G.R.I.T.

Angela Garland

No Money, No Deadline, No Problem

I've always been an entrepreneur. Even as a kid, I was constantly looking for ways to solve problems, hustle, and make things happen with whatever I had. I didn't grow up in a house with structure or order, but I did grow up with ingenuity. That showed up early—like the time I couldn't find a hairbrush before school and used a fork instead. I wouldn't call that a glamorous start, but it says everything about how I move through the world: figure it out, work with what you have, and keep going.

Entrepreneurship was in my blood. My mom was in the shared office industry back in the 1980s—what we now call coworking. She didn't find great financial success in it, but she modeled the tenacity and creativity it took to start something from scratch. That stuck with me.

I went to college right out of high school, but only lasted a semester. I joined a sorority, was a little sister in five fraternities, played intramural sports, worked, spent my entire student loan on party favors, and barely made it to class. I came home, worked for my mom at her new start-up business center, and attended the community college. Once I got my grades up (I was determined to go back to the university), I was accepted back into the university. After another year away from home, freedom, no responsibility, and lots of fun, I finally realized I was not ready at that time to pursue school full-time.

Within a couple of years, I was married and pregnant with my first child. I went back to school and finished my undergrad at 28 while having more babies, waiting tables, teaching aerobics, working retail, and I joined every MLM business under the sun, participated in focus groups, and even acted as a mock patient for a medical school. I did what I had to do to be with my kids and still earn a living. The flexibility I found through those years of patching together work taught me more about business than any classroom ever could.

In the early 2000s, while in my early 30s, I opened my first business center and sold it just a few short years later. During that time, I envisioned a world where small business owners could come to a workspace that had private offices, meeting rooms, shared services, an open seating area, and specialty coffee.

I would finally get to open that business 15 years later at the age of 48. Some people think there's a window for chasing dreams. I've lived enough life to know that the window never actually closes. That belief carried me through more seasons than I can count—through motherhood, burnout, failed partnerships, corporate detours, and messy restarts. I've always been an entrepreneur; I just didn't get to fully embrace my desire and vision because my priorities were my children and making sure they had what they needed.

Turns out, the big vision would not end up where it started. It would come together in a little coffee trailer. On a little street. In small-town Missouri.

By my early thirties, during the summer of 2000, while working full-time and paying childcare for four kids and only getting to be with them for dinner, baths, and bedtime, I was getting impatient. I pitched a business plan for my own shared office center to a local bank president, who just happened to be my best friend's dad. He listened kindly. Then turned me down flat. No personal assets, no collateral, no loan.

But…he introduced me to a few investors. They didn't write checks either, but they gave me advice—and something even more valuable: belief. I didn't need everyone to believe. Just one or two to say, "You've got something here. Keep going."

Eventually, through networking, I found a landlord with vacant space that was fully furnished, with completely wired internet, phones, a meeting room, private offices, and an open mind. I proposed a 50/50 deal; he'd cover expenses, I'd run the business and bring in revenue. It worked, for a while. Then it didn't. So I offered to buy him out—for one dollar more per square foot—and he said yes. Just like that, I owned a business outright. No money exchanged. Just guts and pure determined negotiation.

I never did pay myself until I sold the business. Instead, I made money through consulting in the shared office industry. I helped launch a business center for a large builder and developer in St. Louis, Missouri, as well as various landlords wanting the concept in their buildings.

Again, through networking, a commercial real estate broker connected me to a deal with the state university to develop the first shared office space and technology park on a military installation. This is what gave me the courage to leave the corporate job.

Those two years that I built OffiStart (the shared office concept), I signed up almost 100 virtual office customers and office members. When a buyer approached me two years in, I sold it. Half up front, half in a three-year note. I paid off debt, bought some new furniture, and finally started my MBA—another long-held personal dream I didn't think was possible until it was.

After selling the first business, I started pitching my long-time vision of my "business club" idea to potential investors. My MBA cohorts gave me feedback and perspective on my business plan, and after two years of pitching the idea and being rejected, I reached out to the largest provider of shared office space in the world. I flew on private jets, met with presidents of billion-dollar companies, worked with designers, architects, real estate brokers, and market researchers—all with the hope that I would get to see the vision born.

For a while, I thought this was it: my shot to scale something huge with a corporate partner. But after a year, the project got shelved. Market conditions changed. The CEO wished me well and gave me a severance package. For the second time.

For the first time ever, I was lost. I wasn't sure what I was supposed to do next. My husband was less than supportive and told the kids we would need to start getting the house ready to sell. Instead of being my anchor and telling me it would all work out, he was actually angry. This was the straw that broke the camel's back for me. Within a year, we were separated. We lost our house to foreclosure, and divorce was impending, and I had four teenagers living in an upscale part of St. Louis, Missouri.

After a year of talking to potential investors again and doing some side work and consulting, I came to the conclusion that I needed stability, and it was time to put the idea on the shelf—maybe forever. It was November 2008. I got a corporate job with benefits, a 401(k), a flexible schedule that allowed me to work from home, and an "ok" salary. I thought I'd stay a year; I stayed eight.

What gave me the courage to get back at it was a mountain. Literally. The CEO of Century 21, where I was working, told a story at dinner about a climb he did each year to raise money for charity. I asked if women ever joined the team. He said not that year—and then invited me.

I'd never climbed a mountain. Didn't know what crampons or carabiners were. But I trained with the time I had. I reached out to friends to borrow gear and rented the equipment. I flew to Mexico with a team of five male climbers. I was the only female climber other than one of the guides. Over ten days, I summited the third and seventh highest peaks in North America. It was the hardest thing I'd ever done. And when we reached the summit of the second mountain, exhausted and freezing, I looked at the team and half-joked, "Now that we did this, anyone want to start a business?" Back at the hotel, the CEO asked what I meant. I told him my vision: a new kind of coworking space. One with soul. He told me to start working on it while keeping my job. So I did.

That vision eventually led me to a small town outside St. Louis, Missouri, where no one had heard of coworking and the nearest national coffee chain was inside a large retail chain. My husband and I opened a shared workspace and slowly added specialty coffee—first self-serve, then lattes from an espresso machine we salvaged from a failed café in the same building.

At first, the coffee was just meant to draw people in, to say, "Hey, what's this place?" But what we noticed was that coffee created community. People came for a latte and stayed to talk, to meet, to work. We found that the coffee house was growing, and there were no drive-thru coffee shops in town. There was the opportunity.

Around the same time, I visited my daughter in Washington State and saw drive-thru espresso stands on every other corner. It was a light-bulb moment. Back home, a local veteran was running a drive-up coffee trailer in the parking lot of a nearby town. While my husband examined his trailer and how we might make it two-sided, I worked on finding a lot to put the trailer on.

We found a lot (gravel lot, abandoned gas station, across from a cemetery) and designed our 16 x 8 little orange trailer with windows on both sides. We figured out the car stack and then opened for business. No fast-casual experience. No investors. No backup plan. Just two people in their 50s who believed in good coffee and fast service. Within a week, we were seeing more traffic than our sit-down café had in months.

We opened our second location in March 2020. The next day, the world shut down.

But drive-thru coffee? It was essential. And we adapted fast: touchless transactions, limited menus, long hours. Some staff quit, so my husband and I worked the drive-thru ourselves. It was exhausting, but it worked. We didn't just survive. We grew.

Since then, we've opened 8 locations. We roast our own beans. We make our own syrups. We sell retail bags, support local schools, and donate office space to nonprofits. Our original coworking space now houses our corporate team. The vision changed, but the mission—cultivating real connections through great coffee—stayed the same.

At 48 with four grown kids, two still in college, a new husband, and an hour commute, I decided to open a business in Washington, Missouri, a town of 14,000, and I didn't know a single person in town. I saw a need—a problem that needed to be solved. The coworking business was about bringing home-based workers, start-up ventures, field reps, and consultants all to the same space to work, meet, and have community.

The second business was about another need—no drive-thru coffee for 30 miles.

I didn't start the drive-thru coffee business until I was 51. I had no investors, no trust fund, no big retirement cushion to cash in. No experience in drive-thru. At all.

I've been asked whether entrepreneurs are born or made. I think it's both. Some of us are born with a wild streak: risk-takers, problem-solvers, visionaries. Others learn it through grit and necessity. What I know for sure is this: You don't need perfect timing. You don't need a pile of money. You don't need anyone's permission.

You need a dream worth waiting for, and the guts to chase it when the moment comes.

So if you've hit pause because life got in the way—babies, bills, burnout—don't give up. Put the dream on a shelf if you must, but don't throw it away. Dust it off when you're ready.

Find a new window if the first one closes or never opens.

I'm living proof of that.

Angela Garland is the CEO, co-founder, and owner of Exit 11 Coffee, a spin-off from Exit 11 Workspace, which was founded in 2015. They now own and operate 8 drive-thru coffee shops, a coffee roasting facility, and the original coworking center.

Angela began her career assisting small business owners working for international shared office and coworking companies. Her first start-up, OffiStart Business Centers, was sold in 2004. She served for many years as a real estate franchise consultant and coworking consultant. She earned her undergrad and MBA 10 years apart while raising 4 children. She was married the first time for 20 years and now 10 years with her husband and business partner, Scott.

Angela likes her wine and time with friends as much as she likes her coffee. And her most exciting adventure of late is enjoying her four grandchildren: Elijah, Ruby May, Isabel, and William.

Please scan the QR code to connect with this author.

G.R.I.T.®

Zellipah Githui

My Immigrant
Entrepreneurship Journey

I was born in a large family. I am the 16th child out of 17 of my father, and eighth of nine of my mother. Being raised in a large family and in a country where people hang out, eat, share, and play together meant I was used to being with people all the time.

Ever since I was a little girl, I have dreamt of having a distribution center. As I grew up, the idea came twice. Growing up in rural Kenya, I saw a lot of poverty and defined what success meant to me. I defined it as "having a large distribution center in Kenya, which created employment for a lot of people, so they can feed their families and improve their livelihood."

As I was graduating in food science and post-harvest technology in Kenya, one professor asked us to write what we wished to do with our education. Without thinking twice, I wrote that I wanted to have a very large distribution center that created employment for a lot of people. It would manage the supply of farm produce from remote farm areas of production to urban or other areas where there was a shortage.

I left my home country of Kenya in early 1998 to continue my education with a hope of returning after two years. I desired to get a master's in business administration, so I relocated during the middle of winter to a small town, a much quieter, lonely place where few people looked like me. I moved to Pittsburg, Kansas. Go Gorillas!

I remember my first few days in Pittsburg like it was yesterday. It was sunny outside. When I see the sun, I think of warmth. The morning after my arrival, and in my naivety, I decided to take a walk to enjoy the sun and wear down the jet lag, wearing a t-shirt without a winter coat. As I walked, my body was communicating with me in an unfamiliar language. My lips were shaking as I walked even faster to try to enjoy the sun. I met a couple that were fully layered up in long coats. The couple stopped and asked me if I was an international student, to which I responded in the affirmative. They asked if I had a jacket, and I told them I had a jacket in the hotel room. They told me to go back to the hotel and get my jacket.

Without questioning that authority, I turned back, and at this time, my body was now quite numb. The room was warm, I wore the jacket, and now I could feel myself again. Were these early symptoms of hypothermia? That's how my life began in the United States as an immigrant.

A few days later, I left my hotel and moved into my dorm room. Let me say nothing made sense. The dorm life, the cafeteria, the teaching style, the loneliness. People moved in and out.

No one talked to me, no one could understand me, even when I spoke perfect English. I got questions like: "Are you speaking Spanish?" "Did you live in trees in Africa?" "How did you come here?" "Did you come by boat?" It was a true culture shock.

Month one, month two, month three, I had almost lost myself to depression. I used to cry a lot at night. Worse still, I could not reach my parents or siblings as there were no cell phones back then. Landlines were scarce in Kenya, and one needed to schedule to talk to someone ahead of time. As I am writing now, tears still roll down my face because it feels just like yesterday.

In March of the same year, in desperation, I went to the university's International Students' Office. I had a suitcase of souvenirs gifted to me by my nieces as a remembrance since they worried that I'd not return home to Kenya. I explained to the office that I needed to showcase my culture with these gifts. The office approved me to set up a table in the dining hall.

Very expeditiously, I started communicating. Oh, it felt good. I could be understood as well as I understood them. When the people asked if I could sell the items, I was so happy as my entrepreneurship kicked in. I sold souvenirs. I started selling earrings for two dollars. One person recommended that I raise the price to five or six dollars. Clearly, I had no idea how much they were worth. Remember, they were gifts, and I am in a new country and a new market. The joy of feeling right at home, comfortable, and gaining myself back was real. Another student informed me of a festival called the Fourth of July, and another student told me about the Little Balkans Day Festival that happens on Labor Day.

The gifts had become my medium of communication. I learned very quickly that what got me here will not sustain and get me there. Nothing has humbled me like migrating to the United States. I had a family, career, friends, professional connections, and all the perks that came with it. I had to start from scratch. I also had learned that I was black, an immigrant woman, and that meant I had to carry myself differently.

The Fourth of July came, and sure enough, I was a vendor. I rolled out my suitcase of souvenirs and arranged them on the floor just as they did back home. Customers came and supported me quite a bit. By the end of day one, I had enough money to purchase a table and a tent.

On day two, the vendor next to me helped me organize my items, and I had a better selling experience. I continued going to festivals, powwows, and holiday craft fairs at schools, malls, and churches. With each setup, I saw the opportunity to support artisans like my mother and others back home. I started ordering more handcrafts while still at the dorms, until summer came, and I rented a studio apartment.

My goal now became finding a way to share the beautiful work of the artisans with others in a way guaranteed to benefit everyone involved in a fair and prosperous way. I started Gitzell Imports LLC (Gitzell Fairtrade International). I focused on craft fairs, festivals, and later, wholesale with the purpose of making a difference and real impact on the producers in Third World countries.

I had learned the art of weaving from my mother when I was a little girl. It was a chore among others, like knitting, milking, and sewing. I seemed to prefer it over others. As I continued with my home décor business, I started inclining towards selling artisan-made baskets.

I was still in college, and as I graduated with a Master's in Business Administration (MBA), I also graduated to be called a mother. Juggling single motherhood and owning a business that required a lot of travelling on weekends was not easy. It required pivoting from my then almost four-year-established business.

I also had learned that I quickly needed to adapt to the American system if I was going to be successful. I needed to learn how systems work and how they interact with each other. I equipped myself with an understanding of the immigration system, education, credit, business, you name it, I learned it all. I also decided that I will not confuse movement with progress, and I need to be strategic and grounded in my new country of residence.

I needed to focus on employment to provide stability for me and my son. Though it took four years to land my career in corporate America, I worked in this space for 17 great years in research and development, quality management, compliance, and logistics with one of the largest agricultural research firms in the world. It's in this company that I must admit that I worked with some of the greatest minds this world has to offer. The environment also helped build my confidence, tuned my presentation skills at work and with my business, helped me understand systems, but more importantly, being able to bring my authentic self to corporate America was priceless.

It's during my time juggling a career in agricultural research, entrepreneurship, importing home decor, and single motherhood that I reconnected and got married to the love of my life. My husband and son have been my two strong pillars in the growth and operations of the business.

Entrepreneurship has several bumps along the way, and my terrain was no different. African home décor is a niche segment of the entire home decor market. To help with growth and market penetration, I joined the Fair Trade Federation to be a verified member. I also joined local Chambers of Commerce and several women entrepreneur groups. All these groups have been quite helpful in amplifying my business voice.

Born and raised in Kenya, I have taken my love for my culture and my language and created a superpower. My homegrown magical powers have allowed me to show my true authenticity. This makes me both a leader and a powerhouse in the African home decor industry.

Importing from Africa is through a non-standard supply chain, which I refer to as grassroots because the baskets are woven in rural, remote areas. Getting goods to the city or port for export is not always easy. This has turned into an opportunity where I can train other fellow entrepreneurs.

Access to financing remains a main challenge for minority business owners. As a BIPOC entrepreneur, when I show up for an appointment, the lender will most often ask if we are waiting for the owner while skipping my name because no one wants to attempt to read it.

Almighty God has a real sense of humor. He determined that my new type of distribution center would be home décor, located in the middle of the Midwest. Several years later, Gitzell Fairtrade International, with a mission of improving the livelihood of families in Africa, works with mainly female entrepreneur artisans from several African countries. Selling through Gitzell Fairtrade provides artisans with the opportunities that they don't have to travel to the markets. They are assured of the price; they receive a down payment ahead of time so that they can source materials for their crafts and then get paid in full when the pieces are completed. Most of the artisans are also smallholder farmers.

We import these colorful fair-trade baskets and home décor goods and distribute them to our customers, who are mainly retail stores, museums, zoos, and gift shops in North America and Canada. Gitzell Fairtrade is present in more than 1,200 stores. We operate out of our warehouse in Saint Charles, Missouri, with a small staff of five employees. We offer tours and team-building activities in the warehouse as well.

With my entrepreneurship experience, I have been able to create an opportunity to become a guest speaker in diverse areas, one who is dedicated to fostering personal and professional growth. I'm a staunch advocate for entrepreneurship and business scaling, recognizing the transformative potential they hold for individuals and communities alike.

I write this anthology chapter in honor of my mother, who juggled smallholder farming, selling a little extra produce, and supplementing with weaving baskets to provide for us. As I am pursuing my PhD in Business Management, I honor my father for instilling in me the discipline of education. To my North Star, my son, my life partner, my family, including my nieces, whose gifts I sold, I salute you all. Honor and glory go to God.

Zellipah Githui is the founder of Gitzell Fairtrade International, a social impact brand. She is a dynamic force with a solid background in International business, quality management systems, and several years' experience in agriculture, manufacturing, and nonprofit management.

Driven by her passion for making a meaningful impact, Zellipah is a speaker who is deeply committed to enhancing local and global communities. She believes in the power of storytelling to shed light on important issues such as immigrants' experiences, justice, diversity, equity, inclusion, and entrepreneurship. She is a catalyst for positive change, inspiring others to join her in building a brighter, more equitable future for all.

In 2021, she was awarded the St. Louis Immigrant Entrepreneur Award and the prestigious Marquis Who's Who. In 2024, she was awarded the Family Business of the Year, and in 2025, the African Business of the Year.

She is a board member of the Fair Trade Federation, the United Nations Association of Saint Louis, and the African Chamber of Commerce, St. Louis. She lives in St. Louis with her family, and they love to travel.

Please scan the QR code to connect with this author.

G.R.I.T.

D'Von Johnson

Painting with Purpose

I wasn't born with a silver spoon in my mouth. I came from poverty, where the odds were stacked against me—where stories like mine usually end in statistics, not success. My story doesn't start with connections, funding, or an Ivy League degree. It starts with grit. With making things work when they shouldn't have. With figuring out how to eat, how to survive, and eventually, how to build. I come from a place where you either hustle or you get left behind. There weren't many safety nets. Growing up, I watched family members stretch food, hold down multiple jobs, and make something out of nothing. I learned to be resourceful, to adapt, and to never make excuses. I also saw what happened when people gave up. I decided early that I wouldn't be one of them.

The road to entrepreneurship wasn't a clear one. I wasn't raised around business owners. No one handed me a blueprint. But I always had a vision for something greater. I didn't want to just survive—I wanted to build a life with meaning. I wanted to create opportunities for myself and others. I wanted to prove that someone from my background could make it, not by chance, but by choice.

Starting D. Johnson Painting was my leap of faith. I had no investors, no formal training in business, and no safety net. What I had was a commitment to excellence and a work ethic that didn't stop. I knew how to paint, and I knew how to treat people right. That was my foundation. In those early days, I did it all—cold calling, knocking on doors, painting until my hands were sore, then staying up late to work on invoices and proposals. I learned on the fly. I made mistakes, but I always learned from them. I studied pricing, perfected my craft, and built a reputation for showing up and following through. There were weeks when I questioned if it was worth it. But every time I thought about quitting, I thought about why I started.

I started for the kid in me who once thought success was out of reach. I started for the people in my community who needed to see that it's possible. I started because I believed that creating something from scratch would give me the power to not only change my life but also impact others. As D. Johnson Painting grew, so did I. I learned how to build a team, how to scale systems, and how to lead with intention. I realized that entrepreneurship isn't just about being in control—it's about being responsible. You carry the weight of others' livelihoods, expectations, and trust. I take that seriously.

There were breakthroughs along the way: the first time I landed a large contract, the first time I hired a crew I didn't have to micromanage, the moment I realized the business could operate without me swinging a brush. These were milestones that reminded me how far we had come.

Recognition followed. We were honored with the MOKAN Emerging Business Award. I was named an Emerging Leader by the Construction Forum, received the Rising Star Award from the St. Louis Council of Construction Consumers (SLC3), and was recognized by *Small Business Monthly* as one of its Heroes in Business. Each award felt like validation—not just of my work, but of the journey. A reminder that even if you start at a disadvantage, you can still rise. But success to me isn't just defined by awards or revenue. It's defined by impact.

One of the proudest parts of running D. Johnson Painting is our community work. Every year, we organize a toy giveaway that reaches hundreds of families. We invest in youth through mentorship programs, school visits, and speaking engagements. I never wanted to be the guy who made it and left his people behind. I wanted to be the example that says, "You can make it and still show up for your community." Giving back isn't just something we do—it's part of our DNA. I've been that kid who needed to see someone doing it right. I've been the young man looking for guidance, for proof that there's another way. If I can be that for someone else, then every long night, every tough lesson, and every sacrifice is worth it.

And there were sacrifices. Entrepreneurship is not all freedom and flexibility. There were times I couldn't sleep from the stress and missed personal events because I had to handle a job site, and times I doubted myself, wondering if I was built for this. But what I've learned is that success is a battle of endurance more than talent. If you can outlast the hard times, the wins will come.

There was a stretch when I was working sixteen-hour days, six and sometimes seven days a week. I remember eating lunch in my van between site visits, running payroll on my phone while standing in paint-splattered clothes, trying to keep the vision alive. There were no breaks, just belief. I had to sacrifice comfort for growth. I had to grow faster than the business. And in the midst of it all, I had to fight the self-doubt that creeps in when things don't go your way, like losing a bid you thought you had or getting ghosted by a client after a walkthrough. I've stood in the middle of a half-finished job wondering how I was going to keep everything together. But every time, I did. Every time, I figured it out. Because I refused to be another story that *almost* made it.

The truth is, I've failed. I've lost money. I've hired the wrong people. I've overextended myself. But I've also gotten back up every single time.

That's what separates those who dream from those who build. It's not perfection—it's persistence. What a lot of people don't see is the internal work—the emotional toll of leadership, the pressure of being responsible not only for your future, but for the livelihood of your team. I had to grow spiritually and mentally. I had to become a better communicator, a better listener, and a better version of myself. Building a business stretched me, sharpened me, and made me look inward more than I ever expected.

To anyone reading this, wondering if entrepreneurship is for you, understand this: It will test everything you think you know about yourself. It will force you to grow, to change, to stretch. But it will also give you something no one can take away: ownership. Not just of a business, but of your story. You don't need a perfect plan to get started. You need courage. You need discipline. You need purpose. The rest, you can figure out along the way. I'm living proof of that.

D. Johnson Painting is more than a company. It's a movement. It's a reminder that where you start doesn't determine where you finish. That hustle, vision, and heart can build something real. That you can come from poverty and still create a legacy. I used to dream of stability. Now I dream of scale—of how we can impact more lives, employ more people, and inspire more entrepreneurs to bet on themselves. If my story can help someone else start theirs, then this journey is already a success.

And we're just getting started.

The next chapter for D. Johnson Painting is about scale and sustainability. We're not just painting spaces—we're creating opportunity. I want to hire more people from the same neighborhoods I came from. I want to show young men and women that a trade can lead to ownership. That you don't have to leave your city to build a future—you can build it right where you are. In the years ahead, I see us growing into new markets, training future leaders, and continuing to pour into the community that shaped me. I want to expand our workforce development efforts, partner with schools and nonprofits, and build a model that other minority-owned businesses can follow.

If there's one thing I know for sure, it's that legacy doesn't happen by accident. It's built with intention—choice by choice, day by day. My name is D'Von Johnson, and this is just the beginning of what I hope will be a long, purpose-driven journey of impact through entrepreneurship.

This is more than a business—this is legacy in motion.

Looking back, I can honestly say that building this business saved my life. It gave me purpose at a time when I needed it most. It forced me to level up—not just as a professional, but as a man. Every lesson, every setback, and every victory has been part of a larger transformation. I'm not the same person who started out with a paintbrush and a dream. I've grown into someone who understands the weight of responsibility and the beauty of purpose. And I carry that with me into every room I walk into.

So, whether you're standing at the starting line or already deep in the trenches of your own journey, I hope this chapter encourages you. Keep going. Keep believing. Keep building. Because one day, your story might be the spark that lights the way for someone else.

D'Von Johnson is the founder and owner of D. Johnson Painting, a minority-owned painting company based in St. Louis, Missouri. A Black entrepreneur who rose from poverty, D'Von built his business on a mission of excellence, resilience, and service. He has been honored with the MOKAN Emerging Business Award, the Rising Star Award from the St. Louis Council of Construction Consumers (SLC3), recognized as an Emerging Leader by the Construction Forum, and named one of *Small Business Monthly's* Heroes in Business.

Beyond entrepreneurship, D'Von is deeply committed to his community—organizing annual toy drives, mentoring youth, and championing equity in the trades. His story is one of purpose, perseverance, and creating a legacy rooted in impact. When he's not working, D'Von enjoys exploring new ideas and investing in the growth of others.

Please scan the QR code to connect with this author.

G.R.I.T.

James Maher

Taking Care of Families™

The youngest son of four children, I was the fifth generation of an Irish farming family raised outside of Des Moines, Iowa. My maternal grandparents were the fourth Italian family to settle in Des Moines. Dad would often joke, "You have enough Italian in you to *want* to fight, and enough Irish to *know* how!" My father was an incredibly hard worker who served in the Army during the Korean War. After completing service, he returned home to work on the family farm. In 1966, he started his own farm, where he was an innovator with agricultural livestock production. Mom worked as a registered nurse for the VA. Her mother passed away when she was seventeen, leaving her father to raise her and two younger sisters, who were fifteen and twelve at the time.

My wife's paternal family immigrated from Austria and settled in East Saint Louis. My father-in-law was an executive at IBM, working in Saint Louis. After retiring, he spent fifteen years working for a privately held company headquartered in Belleville, Illinois. My mother-in-law was of German descent. She worked as a kindergarten teacher and raised a family while working in the physical therapy department at a local hospital.

This background is important for understanding my family. My wife and I met in 1990 and were married in 1992. We both come from hardworking families and share values of education, a strong work ethic, and dedication to our careers.

At thirty years old, my values were the foundation and requirements I was set to build upon to provide for my family. And nothing was going to stop me. As life rolled forward, there came increasing growth and responsibility. With my head down and in retrospect, selfishly, I poured all my time and energy into my career, working ninety-plus-hour weeks. I traveled ninety-five percent of the time to rural communities, working for the first broker-affiliated trust company with federal trust powers. Starting the trust company four years before, I continued to build the business. I also ran an in-home law practice, providing estate planning services for the needs of the company's employees. I worked long hours, speaking to advisors, holding client meetings, presenting at community town halls, and meeting with attorneys and CPAs in the communities to educate them about our services that were now available. I wanted to be on the partnership track, thinking that was my path forward.

On September 24, 1996, my life was changed forever—for the better. Until that point in my life, I believed I had been living with clarity of purpose and mission. I had well-defined values and goals… and I thought I was living by them—until my life seemed to stop. It was the day my first son was born. I became a father and my wife a mother. Together, we became parents. He is my namesake, James Donald Maher Jr., whom we immediately nicknamed "JD."

We brought JD home from the hospital with jaundice. It was a common condition seen in newborns. His doctors recommended an at-home treatment with a bilirubin suitcase that looked like a miniature tanning bed. He wore little goggles, and we laid him under the lights to treat his jaundice.

When we took our son for his first checkup three days later, his bili-rubin numbers were *really* high, and they continued to climb higher. The pediatrician knew this was something more serious and immediately admitted JD to the hospital for testing.

It *was* something more.

We were fortunate. Our pediatrician had seen the condition before, and because of her experience, JD received early treatment. If he hadn't received treatment within his first six weeks of life, the mortality rate for newborns with his condition would have been nearly one hundred percent. The fear I felt was immense.

Within three weeks of his birth, JD was officially diagnosed with a disease called Biliary Atresia, a rare liver disease that affects newborns.

At that point, I was still working, trying to juggle both work and family, splitting my time between the office and hospital with my wife and son. I had a choice to make; I couldn't continue a career traveling most weeks. I needed to be home with my family. I decided to change roles within the company to one that no longer required me to travel.

As I read the medical journals at night while staying with my wife and son at St. Louis Children's Hospital, I learned the one-year mortality rate for these children was nearly ninety percent prior to 1989. Then, a team at the University of Chicago successfully split an adult liver into two lobes. One lobe was dissected from a living adult patient and was transplanted into the infant. Worldwide, only about 400 procedures had been done at that point. In fact, it had never been done in Saint Louis! The term "living donor" was coined from this type of procedure.

The balance of JD's life was literally in our hands. We were new parents and had been married just days shy of four years when this defining moment occurred.

There was hope—a living donor transplant! To be a candidate for a living donor transplant, you have to be a match with the patient. I decided to be tested to see if I was a match for JD. I went through weeks of continuous testing, and thankfully, I was a match! That's when everyone started weighing in. Both our families were concerned about the risk of mortality this presented to the living donor and recipient. There came a point when, as young parents, we determined this was our decision—not theirs.

We decided to have the surgeons at the University of Chicago perform the transplant, and JD received the left lobe of my liver on June 2, 1997. It was a success!

Following his initial surgery, he was in the ICU for twenty-eight days. There were several points in time when we questioned whether or not we had made the right decision, because of all the tubes and monitors, and all the units of blood he was going through. But little by little, his color came back, and we knew the liver was working—he just needed time.

During his stay at the University of Chicago Wyler's Children's Hospital, he needed blood—a lot of blood! It all had to be type A-positive. In preparation for his transplant, we hosted a blood drive and shipped one hundred units of blood to Chicago for JD. Within fourteen days, he had practically gone through the entire one hundred units!

The doctors said he was going to need continued blood transfusions for the foreseeable future. I told them I would get more, and the medical team laughed and said, "The one hundred donors who gave at your initial blood drive can't give blood within sixty days." I replied, "We will get another one hundred units of blood—you don›t know me."

And I did it!

I made calls, and we hosted another blood drive. We shipped another one hundred units of blood, and that lasted JD another fourteen days. He received two hundred units of blood in the twenty-eight days following surgery. It was crazy! He remained in Chicago for his care. I traveled back and forth for work, as I had just started a new role within the company a couple of months earlier.

Throughout this experience, I witnessed true suffering and endurance from JD—nothing less than inspiring. How could he, so young and small, be *so* determined to live? How could he be willing to fight, with everything he had, at such a young age?

He came home from the hospital three months later; he was thriving. He was physically growing and beginning to develop the motor skills that he had been lacking. Slowly but surely, he was catching up. His doctors routinely monitored his condition, and around age five, they discovered an issue with the blood flow to JD's liver. Scar tissue had developed in a vessel that supplied JD's liver with blood. Every six weeks, for two years straight, we would spend a week in the hospital with JD in Chicago. They would balloon-open the clogged vessel. The procedure took all of fifteen minutes to perform; however, JD had a severe reaction to the contrast dye that was used for the procedure, forcing him to stay in the hospital for a full week following the procedure.

By that time, our family had grown to include three boys: JD at five years, a two-year-old, and a newborn baby. For JD's well-being and our family's quality of life, he was put on Chicago's transplant list, where he remained for the next two years without gaining any status. Looking for alternative options, we visited Atlanta and met with a young, energetic, and experienced doctor who was confident in JD's outcome for a second transplant. JD was switched to the transplant list at Emory University in Atlanta, Georgia. He received a new liver after waiting just three months on the list in Atlanta.

Sometimes, grit is developed, not where you would envision, but through an experience that has forever changed you. True grit, in my mind, emerges not as how one works, but why they work. My son's journey deepened my faith-first mentality: God is always listening, and this experience forever embedded the importance of family. It led me to trademark the phrase, "Taking Care of Families™," when I founded our company, Archford, in 2013.

After a long career and so many interactions with individuals faced with terminal illnesses, I have found that most terminal peoples' thoughts and intentions are centered around their loved ones and future generations. "Taking Care of Families™" emphasizes helping others, becoming more, and sharing success, which are our core values, and is why I do what I do every day. This mission, influenced by my family's experience, remains at the core of my work today. It drives me to help families preserve their identity and maintain harmony. The importance of these two (faith and family) can enable great things as one looks for that inner spirit to fuel their grit!

As parents, witnessing JD's arduous journey and the empathy it instilled in his younger brothers fostered a deep appreciation for resilience within our family. As they grew up watching JD get stuck with needles routinely, they developed compassion at an early age, because it was normal life for them. The courage JD displayed is undeniable, and his fighting spirit became a source of inspiration. His dedication has instilled a deep understanding of grit in his younger brothers, inspiring them to excel academically and athletically, even at a professional level in sports.

Through it all, JD's journey has been one of strength and perseverance, echoing the determination seen in our family roots. He grew up to embody the grit that shaped him, eventually graduating from the University of Missouri in 2019 with Magnum Cum Laude honors in finance. In 2022, he earned his J.D. from the School of Law at the University of Missouri, and in 2025, he received his Master's Degree from Indiana University Lilly Family School of Philanthropy, proving that the hurdles he faced only fueled his resolve.

JD's journey will forever inspire us. Today, my wife and I are proud to see him join Archford, where he is working with our family office team, bringing with him the core value of "help others," that has been rooted in him through his unique life experiences. Every day, his drive and determination motivate us to fulfill our mission with the same tenacity and spirit that he has always exemplified.

My calling in life is to be a father—a role that has enriched my understanding of what it means to care for families. In entrepreneurship, my source of strength and insight came from JD's incredible journey. As I work towards preserving family harmony and supporting others, I am constantly reminded of the grit and determination JD demonstrated. It is this understanding that allows us to truly comprehend and serve the families who are at the heart of our business.

James, an attorney and CPA, holds a bachelor's degree and a law degree from the University of Missouri–Columbia. He is the CEO and founder of Archford. Believing the most important asset for business owners is the employee, James's goal is to assemble an extraordinary team.

James's seven designations, including Certified Financial Planner, allow him to design financial and tax-advantaged plans. An award-winning, nationally recognized authority in estate planning, business transition, and philanthropy, he is a sought-after speaker and thought leader.

He is a member of the Missouri Bar, National Center for Employee Ownership, Vistage, St. Louis Titan 100 Hall of Fame, Exit Planning Institute, and Leadership Council of Southwestern Illinois.

James and his wife, Jenny, have four sons who are a source of unparalleled joy, each marked by their unique achievements, humility, and resilience.

Please scan the QR code to connect with this author.

G.R.I.T.

Alison Martin

Failing Forward

We often see people standing confidently on the other side of success and assume their journey must have been easy—or that success happened overnight. What we don't often see are the moments of doubt, the obstacles overcome, and the silent sacrifices behind closed doors. As I reflect on my life and career, I see how every chapter, even the most painful ones, prepared me for the next. Nothing about my path was linear. Nothing about it was easy. And yet, every experience became part of the foundation on which I would eventually build a purpose-driven business that is transforming lives.

My early life was filled with challenges that shaped me long before I ever knew what entrepreneurship even meant. I dropped out of high school at 16. By 17, I was legally emancipated. By 18, I was a single mom navigating a world that didn't come with a manual. Those years were difficult, but they taught me resourcefulness, grit, and a level of determination I hadn't yet learned to name. Looking back, those traits would become the cornerstones of my future success.

Despite the odds, I became the first person in my family to attend college. I earned my Bachelor's degree in Business Management with highest honors at the age of 24—all while raising my young son. It wasn't just about education; it was about rewriting the narrative I had been handed. By the time I was 29, I was serving as the executive director for a large voluntary health organization, managing a multimillion-dollar fundraising campaign, and leading a board of 23 members. I had no idea at the time, but I was already laying the groundwork for my entrepreneurial journey.

Every entrepreneur has that moment—the spark, the seed of an idea that won't go away. For me, it happened while running a national campaign focused on women's heart health. I found myself surrounded by dynamic, philanthropic women—executives, entrepreneurs, community leaders—who generously offered their time, wisdom, and mentorship. I was just shy of 30, balancing my demanding role while raising an 11-year-old son and a 5-year-old daughter. The guidance I received from these mentors was transformative. It planted a seed that would eventually grow into a bold vision: What if more women—especially those navigating major life transitions like single motherhood, career pivots, or college graduation—had access to that kind of mentorship?

That idea became the foundation for a nonprofit organization I launched, focused on delivering mentorship to underserved women. But as we started building the program, we quickly ran into a challenge: we needed a way to efficiently and meaningfully match mentors and mentees. When I began researching existing software options, none of them met our needs. So, I made a decision that would change everything—I started an LLC, hired a developer, and built a mentoring software platform from scratch.

As we launched the platform within the nonprofit, I began to see its broader potential. Organizations beyond the nonprofit sector were facing the same challenges: how do you scale mentorship? How do you make it meaningful, measurable, and sustainable? In 2015, I made one of the most difficult—and pivotal—decisions of my life. I left my role at the nonprofit I had founded and turned my full focus to building a for-profit company dedicated to helping businesses and associations create impactful mentoring and leadership development programs.

The transition from nonprofit executive to entrepreneur was anything but smooth. Starting a business meant letting go of financial security and embracing ambiguity. I was terrified. I had two kids depending on me. Could I really make this work? Could I handle the pressure of building a company from the ground up? I didn't have all the answers, but I did have clarity on one thing: if I didn't try, I would regret it for the rest of my life. That clarity became my anchor.

I created a lean business plan, established a modest budget, built a basic website, and started having conversations with potential clients. My original vision was to help companies support the advancement of employees through mentorship. But I quickly learned that mentorship was often perceived as a "nice-to-have," not a "need-to-have." The sales cycles were long, sometimes stretching from six months to two years. Many companies deprioritized mentoring programs in favor of initiatives with more immediate ROI. It was disheartening, but not defeating.

Instead of giving up, we refined. We listened. We improved the technology. We used every client interaction, every "no," and every hesitation as a data point. Slowly, we started gaining traction.

Then came 2020—the year everything changed. The pandemic disrupted workforces across the globe. As remote work became the norm, companies scrambled to find ways to maintain culture, support employees, and develop leadership in a virtual environment. That's when our moment arrived. Our mentoring platform was already built for digital delivery. Suddenly, the thing that had once been seen as optional became urgent. Companies needed employee engagement strategies. They needed connection. They needed leadership development—and they needed it virtually.

That was our first major breakthrough. Prior to that, the idea that people could build relationships by phone or by video conferencing was foreign to most, and even though participants could choose to meet in person if they were in the same geography, this had been a significant objection to overcome. This made our program a very attractive option, now that in-person sessions were no longer even possible.

The second breakthrough came when we started listening even more deeply to the root challenges our clients were facing. What they needed wasn't just mentoring. They needed leadership readiness. Too often, organizations were promoting employees into leadership roles without equipping them with the skills to succeed. Succession planning wasn't proactive—it was reactive. We saw an opportunity to position our technology not just as a mentoring tool, but as a strategic solution for leadership development and succession planning. Our program is uniquely positioned to help individual contributors who are not yet responsible for leading a team to expand their worldview by affording them access to leaders for mentoring on leadership skills and by teaching them how to pour into others as a mentor themselves, including college students taking part in our *Aspiring Leaders* program. This is a unique and extremely effective way for up-and-coming talent to not just learn in theory, but also in practice. This is a powerful way to engage current leaders, prepare future leaders, and build a culture where leaders know how to engage and employees know how to approach developmental conversations.

As we honed our value proposition, the business began to scale. But scaling came with its own set of challenges. Hiring the right people, maintaining quality, and building a culture of excellence became my new full-time job. I made many early hiring mistakes—ones that cost us time and energy. At one point, I had to rebuild almost my entire team. It was painful. It felt like a setback. But ultimately, it was the reset we needed. I learned to define roles more clearly, to identify essential skill sets, revamp our sales processes, and redefine our value proposition. The lessons were expensive, but invaluable.

As my company grew, I had to grow too. I could no longer operate as a founder doing everything. I had to step fully into the role of CEO and leader. That meant defining our values, setting the tone for culture, making difficult decisions, and ensuring that every team member was aligned with our mission. Leadership, I learned, isn't about doing more—it's about doing the right things and empowering others to shine.

Our growth strategy has centered around building strategic partnerships with organizations that serve similar audiences but offer complementary services. These collaborations expanded our reach and allowed us to tap into new client pools while maintaining high-impact outcomes. They've also helped us generate a consistent stream of qualified leads, making our sales process more predictable and sustainable.

Because our program is delivered digitally, we are proud to be able to work with companies anywhere, and even prouder to share that our program has been used by employees in over 30 different countries. More than just software, we've created a movement—a new way of thinking about leadership development. The design of the program allows participants to create a learning plan comprised of four essential leadership select topics each quarter and select a mentor to work with them on that topic, and take part in group learning. Over the course of a year, they will develop four critical skills by connecting with mentors both inside and outside of their organization.

But even as a for-profit company, we've stayed true to our roots. Each year, we sponsor college students into our *Aspiring Leaders* program, a mentoring experience that connects students to business professionals to help them prepare for the transition into the workforce. It's our way of paying it forward and continuing to invest in the next generation of leaders.

Looking back, the lessons I've learned along this journey are numerous:

- **Resilience is Everything**—Setbacks will come. The difference between those who succeed and those who don't is the ability to keep going.

- **Failure is a Teacher**—Every mistake holds wisdom. Embrace it. Learn from it. Use it to propel yourself forward.

- **Lifelong Learning is Non-Negotiable**—The world is changing. Staying curious and adaptive is essential to growth.

- **Your Circle Matters**—Surround yourself with mentors, peers, and a team that shares your vision. You can't do it alone.

- **Purpose Fuels Progress**—Money is necessary, but passion and purpose are what keep you going through the tough days.

Entrepreneurship has changed not only my career but my identity. It has tested me, stretched me, and rewarded me in ways I never could have imagined. It's given me the chance to turn my hardships into hope for others. It's brought incredible relationships into my life and allowed me to create something that didn't exist before. Mentorship has been so critical to me throughout my early career and in building my company. Given the challenges I have experienced growing up, I have gotten to experience the transformative impact mentors can have. My first career mentor was a woman by the name of Pat Clary. Pat was the first boss I had who saw my leadership potential and sponsored me into my first executive role, and helped me navigate my early leadership mistakes.

Once I started my company, I turned to seasoned entrepreneurs as mentors. There are so many incredible individuals who come to mind. Sally Tassani helped me have the courage to make the leap as an entre-preneur. Nikki Gregory and Wayne Patrick have both been dear friends, mentors, and powerful connectors. I work with coaches, including Brian Kavicky, who taught me everything I know about sales, and Kristen Miller, who helps me shore up my leadership skills as I build my company. I also had the pleasure of participating in a leadership program where I was very fortunate to be matched with Vicki Mech Hester as my mentor. Vicki has become a most trusted confidante, sounding board, and dear friend.

One of my proudest moments was the first time I received a note from the CEO of a client company who told me our program had profoundly impacted their organizational culture. He included a copy of their annual report and shared that, in no small way, our program had contributed to their successes. He has continued to send something similar each year, and we have now had them as a client for nearly 10 years. That's the kind of impact that keeps me going.

To anyone standing on the edge, contemplating whether to take the leap into entrepreneurship, I offer this: Do it. Trust yourself. You will be challenged. You will be stretched. But you will also be transformed. The path may not be easy, but it will be worth it.

And who knows? The very experiences that once made you feel like an underdog may turn out to be your greatest assets.

Alison Martin is the founder and Chief Program Officer of Engage Mentoring, a firm that helps companies prepare future leaders by providing mentoring and coaching programs for people leaders and high-potential employees. With nearly 20 years in nonprofit leadership—including roles in higher education and as Executive Director for two national health organizations—Alison's passion for talent development led her to launch Engage Mentoring in 2012.

She is the author of *Learning to Lead Through Mentoring* and a recognized thought leader whose insights have been featured in *Authority Magazine*, *Workplace Wellbeing*, *Bizwomen*, and *The HR Director*, among others.

Alison was honored with the Indiana Commission for Women's Torchbearer Award and nominated for Indy's Best and Brightest. She is a frequent speaker at industry conferences and a passionate advocate for expanding access to mentorship.

She is an avid traveler and has been to more than 25 countries. In addition to spending time with her two children, Alison also enjoys paddleboarding and kayaking in her free time.

Please scan the QR code to connect with this author.

G.R.I.T.

Nick Oughton

You Can't Build on Sand

The word "entrepreneur" often feels like a well-worn coin, passed from one business magazine cover to the next, its edges smoothed, and its true value sometimes obscured by overuse. It frequently makes one think of images of a lonely, tired person hunched over a laptop with a glaring screen plastered with an over-packed calendar staring back. However, through my own, sometimes painfully lived experiences, I know this idea falls significantly short of the deep and complex reality it takes to build something from the ground up. Being an entrepreneur is more than just a lonely risk and reward. It involves bringing great people together to help a dream flourish into reality. When dreaming big, you have to understand that it can never be successful with one person. That is not an easy lesson for many—it's one I had to struggle to learn for myself over the years.

Starting my own business was never truly my life's dream. My dream was to make a lot of money and live a good life. Truly, it felt like a simple enough thing to want and to obtain. The money came slowly after school, as it does for most—daily working my nine-to-five, which was increasingly more so because that's the life of Information Technology (IT). But the good life I was searching for didn't seem to come with it. Being frustrated with inconsistent management and having little support for my own successes, I knew it was time to find a different path. I just wasn't sure what that was at the time.

At the time, startup companies weren't a dime a dozen like they appear to be today. So, finding something that people truly wanted or needed wasn't as hard to scrounge up. The iPhone 4 was introduced in 2008, with a sleek glass back that everyone wanted. This fun new glass back had the obvious flaw of cracking or shattering into tiny pieces. Luckily for St. Louis, I believed I was just the person to fix that! I jumped right into the new market and did iPhone and cell phone repairs anywhere I could. Swapping out glass backs for different colors became all the craze for a while. Plus, I was helping to save people's fingers from being cut. From location to location, I went wherever I was needed, working in any space I could find to keep the cash coming in. But even with all the people who needed my services, it wasn't enough to support myself, so this was my side job while working IT elsewhere.

That same year, I had companies approach me about assisting them with their IT needs regularly. How could I say no? The cell phone repairs were easy, but they were not always consistent. This opportunity was something exciting and new—something I could really sink my teeth into… something I could wrangle… something that could all be mine. So, I took on my first three clients and continued blindly forward.

Things stayed consistent for a while, with regular visits to clients who had month-to-month contracts, cell phone repairs here and there, and contract work when and however it came. It seemed like I was finding a niche and gaining my foothold. It felt real and within my grasp. For the first time, I thought I had a base. But that's never how life works out, right?

In 2011, I opened my first shop in St. Louis on Hampton. It was small, but it was everything to me. With a shop, I needed employees to help run it. I had an employee helping with cell phone repairs, but this was nothing like what I had done before. Oh boy, did I *not* know what I was getting into with a team to support and manage! All I knew was that I had to be a better boss and leader than I had at my previous places of employment. I also knew I had to pay them! So, I hired three employees. And off we went into the sun—stretching our wings and feeling the warmth of success on our faces! Or so I thought. Until I turned around and realized that not all my employees had the same vision and drive that I had. They stayed on the ground, holding me from soaring. How could I get them to want to spread their wings and soar with me? I had to show them. I had to make them feel what I felt. I wanted the dream to be alive in *all* of us. How do you get the dream to be alive in them? Make them your friends so they'll be excited with you and do right by you.

Let me tell you, that wasn't what happened, and I'm sure you can figure out why. Not every employee wants to be your friend, and the employees who do want to be your friend sometimes take advantage of that kindness. I constantly struggled on the tightrope of keeping employees happy to not lose everything I had worked for, while simultaneously trying to keep the business running with employees who did not have the drive to keep a small business going. It was a hard lesson to learn, but I understood that I couldn't be everyone's friend, and that's not what they wanted from me. Over time, I built proper boundaries and found ways to still be friendly and kind to employees, without allowing them to feel like they could walk all over me. It took time and a lot of mental reminders on my part, but in the end, it allowed operations to run much smoother.

The years passed, and in 2014, it was time to upgrade the shop. We picked up and moved to a nice place in South County. We continued the iPhone repair along with residential computer repair and sales, and IT support for businesses. I primarily ran on-site to our business clients while leaving the shop in the hands of my employees. Even though there was some uncertainty, I had to let go and learn from any mistakes I encountered along the way. And boy, were there mistakes. Since I had to let go in order to continue supporting business outside of the shop, my employees lacked guidance and were left with their own judgment on things that I should have been involved in. Lacking honest, supportive employees, I didn't know what was going on. The wool was pulled over my eyes, and I had no way of knowing any better.

For two years, things weren't as I tried to make them seem. It felt important to me that the business seemed bigger and more put together than we were at the time. We were always chasing fast cash—taking on any project we could and then going through dry spells for weeks or months. Not enough work was coming in to keep everyone at the hours they were getting. That, in turn, put more work on me, and then I couldn't manage or train employees properly. This wasn't the good life. It felt like it was always nothing but problems. The money wasn't coming. This was not the dream. Where did the dream go?

By 2017, I was stuck in a trick bag and unable to get out; I knew spinning my wheels was getting me nowhere. The next right step was to get a solid foundation beneath me that I could trust, not this feeling of sand falling out from under my feet while I raced to find more sand. It's hard to find good people, and I had to find employees I trusted—more so now after being burned by employees. But even then, it had to get done. I looked for someone I could see real potential in, someone who I could see had my dream's best interest at heart from the very beginning. I tried my luck with the new year in 2018. Spoiler…I found a good one—another employee added to the books, and another day to go on hoping to keep things moving forward. Because now I had someone in my corner, someone I could depend on to help me build the dream. Shedding old ties and figuring out what the next move was, I was hopeful now with someone helping to carry the burden.

Business was good, but always a headache. It was hard being the IT guy for personal technology as well as business technology. The demand was more than we could handle. I had to make a choice, and I knew it wouldn't be easy either way. My business clients had treated me well for years, and I saw the real potential for something different. This could be that real something different I needed.

More years passed, and more employees came and went. Sometimes I rave about the Rule of Eight. It takes eight "meh" (or average) employees before you find that special one who sees the dream. I was fortunate enough to hire two additional core members within a month of each other. Having three strong employees helped me take the dream further and faster than I could have ever imagined—a true base for building the dream and not just sand falling out from under me.

The new core handled the pandemic like they had been through it before. Everyone played his or her part… and then some. This was a big moment for our business, since people had to work from home and started to understand the benefit of proper business security. We took off! As the years really started to sink in, I realized more and more what lessons I had to learn to make it to this point of thriving success in the business. I was no longer chasing fast cash to keep the bills paid. I didn't have to take hold of every little thing and see it through to the end. I didn't have to settle for "meh" employees holding my dream back. I had a base, and that's just the first step.

There are still many lessons to learn along the way and many mistakes to make. But that's the best part of growth—that it's never linear. You have to have the resilience to push through the crazy tug and pull of chasing the dream, knowing that tomorrow the foundation might feel a little stronger than before. Keeping integrity while being beaten down by poor staffing choices, lied to by customers, being fair on all fronts, and keeping a new business together—it's all about being tenacious for the dream and the team that's been built around the dream.

Nick Oughton, a proud St. Louis native, is the founder of NWO IT Services, a managed service provider offering expert IT support to businesses that don't require a full-time internal IT staff.

A dedicated dog lover, Nick is passionate about giving back to local animal shelters and supporting his community in any way he can. His personal and professional life is built on the core values of transparency, honesty, and unwavering dedication, principles that guide how he runs his business and how he engages with people in his life.

These values have earned him recognition as one of the *Top 100 People to Know in St. Louis*. Under his leadership, NWO IT Services has been named among the *Top IT Firms* since 2020 and one of the *Top Cyber Security Firms* since 2022. Nick credits his exceptional team for making these accomplishments possible, consistently upholding the standards that define his vision.

Please scan the QR code to connect with this author.

G.R.I.T.

Jared Peno

There's Nothing Fake About Making It

When I think about grit, I don't think of motivational posters or TED Talks. I think of a 12-year-old car that barely started in the winter. I think of working on a plastic folding table in my basement for five years. I think of being newly married with a newborn baby and no guaranteed paycheck.

In those early years, I had to be the sales team, the service department, the billing guy, the marketing man, and the janitor. I didn't get to "clock out." My life consisted of work, or thinking about work, and hoping that if I put in the hours building it, I could provide for my family's future in a way that I only dreamed of doing. I showed up every day with the same intensity, even when my doubts were louder than my confidence.

Starting out as an entrepreneur was both exhilarating and an exercise in humility. I sold my reliable vehicle and downgraded to something cheaper so I could free up cash while still working at Alliance Technologies to keep my family fed. I had to wake up every day with no salary, very few leads, and no idea where the next check would come from. People think grit is about toughness. Maybe it is. But for me, it is about choosing to believe in something no one else can see yet.

I started my first company, Alliance Technologies, in November 2009. In many ways, though, it was born long before that—in Panera coffee meetings, journal entries, and the discontent felt from my nine-to-five job.

My startup experience might be considered typical for the time, but the changes in technology—and specifically in social media—would lead me to do things differently today. With no clients and no line of credit, my dream was fueled by personal savings and the support from my wife. It's easy to gloss over this part, but everyone should know that without my wife's financial and emotional support, I wouldn't be writing this story. Her support was the number one factor that kept me motivated, growing, and focused.

I am a big supporter of other entrepreneurs, and I tell them all the time that today, you can create a personal brand before you launch and get subscribers before you even have a tax ID. That kind of prep work makes launching a business a much easier proposition than when I started.

Our first client came in just a month after launching, and they're still with us today. There are many success stats I could point to, but that one means the most. I didn't buy my way into this space: it was earned. Slowly. Honestly. And at times, painfully. I often tell people, "Alliance was built, not bought." And when you build something brick by brick, you remember every single piece that went into it.

Every mentor I spoke with said that if you can make it three years, you have a much higher statistical likelihood of succeeding long-term. That's what stuck with me. For some reason, I thought making it three years would unlock some magical door of success. It couldn't have been further from the truth. In fact, I almost didn't make it to year three. I remember being so discouraged one day that I'd decided I'd had enough: becoming an entrepreneur wasn't working, and I was ready to escape back to a 9-to-5.

It was my second year in business. We had a few clients, but it was barely covering our business expenses. Payments for all my hard work were sporadic and very minimal. I felt my family needed me to show up. I had worked on my own for twelve months, like we had planned, and that time was up. My savings were gone, and my wife was financially carrying the family. I felt like every moment I didn't earn, I was letting them down, and we were digging a deeper hole. I admit I didn't handle the pressure well. I hadn't built up the resilience that I have now. In every sales call, I thought they could sense my desperation and knew I was a failure. And why would they do business with a failure?

So, I sat there in that hot car, sweating through my shirt, with tears in my eyes, praying to God to help me. I knew I was called to be a business owner—I could feel it. But in that moment, desperation pushed me to say yes to that interview. Looking around that parking lot, I noticed a sea of nice, reliable cars and people walking in and out from their lunch breaks, chatting and laughing. I was transported back to those days, remembering the comfort, but also recalling the discontent. I knew that life came with asking for permission and settling for what was given to me.

I nailed the interview that I had taken just moments earlier. I knew I'd get an offer. But as I sat there sweating—engine off, a habit formed from never wanting to waste gas—I knew I could never go back to the life of an employee. It just wasn't in my DNA. I never told my wife about that moment; I never told my business partners. With all the sacrifice and hard work everyone had poured into this startup, being here felt treasonous. In this pivotal moment, I was faced with a decision: turn away from eighteen months of grind and let everyone around me down, or find a way to win. I recommitted myself that day, and I've never looked back.

Let's fast-forward ten years. Alliance got over the hump. After a tough start, we landed some key accounts, and the momentum carried us into a thriving business. Pausing growth to maintain our clients would have been a nice lifestyle business. However, the goal was not to replace my job with another. My nature is to build, to explore, and to create. If

I am not moving forward, I am falling behind. Beyond the mission of Alliance, I am personally "not myself" unless I am creating something. I have spoken with numerous entrepreneurs over the years, and many of them describe feeling the same way. This is another reason why I'm dedicated to investing in long-term outcomes: I am building something greater for the version of me in my 50s and 60s. In my experience, if a person carries this kind of passion and vision, good things will happen.

This led me to a taste of success—and the feeling that I had it all figured out. Momentum in a business is a beautiful thing. Once you grab it, you must hang on for dear life because finding it again can take years. One of the greatest momentum killers is losing focus on the thing that got you there. Alliance suffered that fate. We jumped ahead, chasing new business units before mastering the one that finally saw traction. And it cost us. Momentum doesn't break loudly; it slips away quietly, right when your focus does.

We diverted resources—and more importantly, our *attention*—away from our core mission to chase opportunities that never materialized. While we didn't see zero success, the most important lesson it taught me was this: never take your eye off the ball. Because doing so is a momentum killer. The founders hadn't yet worked themselves out of a job, meaning the business still heavily depended on our full attention. We became overleveraged, ineffective, and unfocused. Times were really tough—again.

In addition to all the business setbacks, an unimaginable turn of events led to the death of my business partner, ultimately ushering me into the role of CEO and forcing a quick decision on our next move. The gravity of this moment in my life cannot be understated. I cannot share every detail, so I'll summarize: within a four-month timespan, I endured two funerals, a long-term hospital stay for my critically ill daughter, the breakup of one of my businesses—and to add insult, I totaled my vehicle.

I reflected on that moment in the car ten years earlier, sitting with God for that sweaty thirty minutes of silence, feeling shame, defeat, and loneliness, and toying with the idea of quitting on myself. Here I was, facing another crossroads. I could recommit—or quit.

Over the next two years, I systematically refocused and reignited our team. It required renewed missions, new leadership, new brands, and a bold new strategy to recapture the momentum we once had. The change was painful. I didn't execute flawlessly. I made a lot of mistakes, and I am sure I'm still living with some. I had to let go of the things we poured so much time and money into. I had to break off certain relationships and reorganize the company. The biggest thing I had to do was show up for everyone and lead them through this change. Regardless of my own life circumstances, the team needed me to rally and show them the path to success.

What's simple on paper is entirely different in reality; every great leader knows that they exist to serve their team. My role as a founder has changed dramatically since the early startup days over fifteen years ago. I have delegated many of those roles that I used to own, and I now serve in honor of the team, my partners, and my employees. As CEO of Alliance Technologies and Taligent, I am humbled to be working alongside such great people—each one of them having poured their heart into the mission of our company. I wouldn't be here today without their support.

When I started, I wanted to make it to the three-year mark, like my mentors had said would be the benchmark of success. Now I am focused on playing a much longer game. I promise my team and my clients that I am enduring to be around for the long haul. Operating in this way allows me to avoid short-sighted decisions. I have been at the crossroads of two pivotal moments in my entrepreneurial career. Both were the darkest moments in my life. In each moment, I made the decision to keep moving forward, and each journey thereafter has been punctuated with success.

My resilience in these moments wasn't derived from my own personal well of power and determination. It was only a result of my strong faith in God, and the support from my loving wife Ashlee, that I was able to push through with grit.

I have a long road ahead. As a builder and creator, I relate to so many who have come before me—I'm unable to stop. I think that is part of the entrepreneurial spirit that lives in the vast majority of those who consider themselves entrepreneurs. I will remain active and determined to create value for people, focusing on the *people* part. For all those entrepreneurs out there trying to make it, just remember—it's always darkest right before dawn.

Jared Peno is a husband, father, and follower of Jesus who believes business is a powerful way to serve others and live out your purpose. He values honesty, hard work, and doing what's right, even when it's not easy. For Jared, leadership means taking responsibility, staying grounded in faith, and helping others grow along the way.

That outlook has shaped his journey as an entrepreneur. He co-founded Alliance Technologies and Taligent, two companies focused on helping other businesses thrive through smart technology and people-first support. Jared didn't come from a big corporate background or endless resources; he built things from scratch, with a lot of grit and a clear vision.

Alongside running his companies, he enjoys connecting with other entrepreneurs, offering encouragement, perspective, and real-world advice from someone who's been in the trenches.

Please scan the QR code to connect with this author.

G.R.I.T.

Jackie Robb

Changing Employees' Lives One Project at a Time

I was raised by progressive female trailblazers. My mom and aunt were very family-focused, but also sought fulfillment in the business world of the mid-to-late 20th century. A daunting task to be sure.

Mom joined the Navy during the Korean War as a way out of the marriage/motherhood track of all of the women in her community. Not because she didn't want those things, but she didn't want *only* those things.

Mom and Dad met in the Navy, were married for several years, but separated when I was young. Through hard work and lots of talent, Mom found herself in the advertising world of the Mad Men era. As you can imagine, it was very male-dominated, but Mom fought and managed to rise up in advertising, becoming office manager and finally media specialist. Nearing retirement, she was hired away by a vendor to become a radio station sales manager. After retiring from the radio station, she worked as an independent advertising consultant and managed to travel the world. During her entire career, she was a single mom to me, and I learned so many lessons about life and business from her wonderful example.

My aunt worked her way through night school, getting her business degree from Duquesne University in Pittsburgh, Pennsylvania, and heading off into the business world. She bumped into the "glass ceiling" many times in the male-dominated world of insurance. In a not-unfamiliar scenario, she was passed over for promotion several times by a less experienced man who "had a family to feed." She crisscrossed the country from Pittsburgh, Pennsylvania, to Baltimore, Maryland, to San Francisco and L.A., California, finally landing in Dallas, Texas, as the head of Benefits and Insurance for an international corporation. Naturally, she made less than her male predecessor. Parkinson's disease, unfortunately, robbed her of her later career years, but she went out at the top of her field.

Both of these amazing women were warriors with strong moral convictions. That is what I wanted to emulate.

I was raised with statements like "when you go to college" and "when you decide what to study in college" in a family where no one had ever gone to college straight out of high school. I never thought about it being unusual; it was just how it was. I was going to be a college graduate.

My family likes to tell this story over and over about a day I was playing "office" with two female cousins. My older cousin said she wanted to be an executive secretary. I was overheard to say that's what I wanted to be. Everyone thought I meant executive secretary, but I clarified: I wanted to be an executive. My younger cousin (who went on to graduate college as an adult and is an accomplished RN) asked what she could do. I replied, "Send us a résumé and we'll see what we can do."

Although humorous, for years, I struggled with the apparent callousness of my remark. I had been around when my mom was discussing hiring people for the ad agency where she worked as a manager, or when my aunt was trying to rise up in the insurance industry of the 1960s and 1970s, so I knew what a résumé was. But I hated the idea that I was flippant with my cousin and seemed to push her aside with a platitude. It wasn't until I made the leap into business ownership years later that I found the actual meaning in my words and my true fulfillment.

Yes, I have always been a rebel, a joiner, and a leader. I was the only girl on my middle school newspaper, and I was the feature writer. In high school, I was the editor of the senior section of our yearbook, a senator on the student council, assistant stage manager of our senior class play, vice president of the pep squad, the only female member of the computer club, and president of my homeroom for all four years. As an adult, I served for many years on our city's Planning and Zoning Commission, held many offices in the local chapter of the Hazardous Materials Managers organization, and served on the council at our church.

My public high school in Pittsburgh, Pennsylvania, had an amazing scholars' program and encouraged a bunch of kids from a blue-collar neighborhood to reach for the stars. Of the many professional career paths presented to us, I chose engineering. At the same time, being a child of the seventies, I wanted to save the planet. In 1980, there were no college environmental engineering programs. I decided that, as a mining engineer, I could work on the reclamation of former surface and under-ground mines. So off I went to Rolla, Missouri. My freshman class in Mining Engineering, of one hundred or so students, included only three women. I was proud to be one of them.

During college, I worked as a co-op student in the environmental lab for a strip mine in Pinckneyville, Illinois. We collected soil and surface run-off samples from the mine property and analyzed them in-house. I thought I had found my niche.

I completed my degree at the University of Missouri-Rolla (now MS&T), graduating with ten other students in mining. I was the only woman.

Interviewers came to campus, and that was an eye-opener. Although they honored the interview slots I had signed up for, mining companies told me directly that I would never be hired to work in an underground mine, as the men would not accept a woman underground. It also became clear to me that I was a big city kid and really didn't want to live the rural life that came with jobs in mining, even if I could get one. I didn't know what to do. The career I had studied for was slipping through my fingers.

After college, I moved to St. Louis, Missouri, and found a job with a geotechnical firm performing compaction testing in the field and physical analysis in the laboratory. Soon, my leadership talents were put to use as supervisor of the field and laboratory. My skills at puzzles like Tetris were put to the test, juggling the technicians, field equipment, and site locations to maximum effect. I loved it. I grew my knowledge of drafting (non-computer aided; yes, I'm that old), and thought I had again found my niche.

One day, the owner of the company walked into my office and asked if I'd be interested in doing environmental reports. Hot dog! My desire to save the planet had come full circle. I jumped at the chance, not knowing I would be thrust into the exciting, but still developing, world of Phase I Environmental Site Assessments (ESA).

Phase I ESAs have matured greatly since that time in the mid-80s, and I was along for the ride. With that came other environmental consulting learning opportunities such as soil, groundwater, and wastewater sampling and reporting; underground storage tank removal; management of hazardous materials; and remediation, to name but a few.

In time, I was able to manage an environmental engineering department of a local consulting firm and found I loved training and mentoring new co-workers in the environmental field.

I married the love of my life and had the child of our dreams. I was fortunate to have a loving and supportive partner in my husband, Wes, and was able to continue in my career while we raised our son, Owen. I met Wes as he owned a mobile analytical laboratory that became a vendor. Eventually, he became a co-worker and we were able to carpool to work together, dropping and picking up Owen from school most days. That was a true blessing.

I enjoyed my thirty-year career in environmental consulting as an employee, but as they do, things started to change. My body was not keeping up with the demands of my career as it once did. My knees, which had been bad since college, were making walking and standing exceedingly difficult for me. I wanted knee replacements, but my weight stood in the way. Eventually, with no new job in hand, I tendered my resignation and determined to lose the weight and get new knees.

A friend and previous co-worker and I decided to step out on our own and open an environmental consulting firm in April 2019. It was a thrilling yet terrifying time. With only our experience and network of fellow environmental professionals, we jumped into the unknown. By the end of 2019, we had found a handful of projects and were starting to pick up steam.

Then March 2020 arrived. The world changed. The few environmental jobs we had became fewer, and we wondered if we could survive. My business partner had, along with her environmental degree and experience, run a small construction company consisting of her and a laborer. She noted that, with everyone stuck at home due to the lockdown, her phone was blowing up with requests for home projects. So, we transformed into an environmental *and* construction company.

Our flexibility allowed us to weather the initial few years of the pandemic, but it became clear that we were operating two vastly different businesses. In 2022, we decided to part ways, with my former partner taking the construction side of the business and me retaining the environmental side.

The year before we split up the company, a dear friend, Donna Parks Ratkowski, retired from a lengthy environmental career in chemical manufacturing. Donna had started working part-time for our firm, so it was a natural fit for Donna and me to become equal owners in our newly named company, R&R Environmental Partners LLC.

R&R has grown to be a robust team of environmental, health, and safety professionals who have a vast array of experience in both industry and consulting. Employees of R&R are afforded flexibility that usually only comes with business ownership, without them having to worry about the business side of things like insurance, taxes, marketing, etc. This flexibility that we offer our employees creates a collaborative working environment, with employees taking on projects that suit their skills, preferences, and personal schedules.

It is here, in this partnership, that I have finally found true fulfillment. On a daily basis, we are blessed to be able to provide a safe, non-discriminatory work space for talented and unique individuals. It is like our church says, "All are welcome here."

When a former construction employee reached out to see if we had any handy-person work for them, it was gratifying to have the freedom that comes with business ownership to expand our services to include repair and maintenance services again.

I am finally implementing my "send us a résumé and we'll see what we can do" mindset from many years ago. Being a problem solver is my natural wheelhouse. I love the puzzle aspect of combining the best people with the knowledge, skill, and experience to serve the varied needs of our treasured clients.

Who knew that, at this late stage of my career, I would really and truly find my niche?

I wrote this chapter to honor four people in my life, two who gave me roots and two who give me wings.

My mom, Rose Marie Griggs, and her sister, my late Aunt Ramonda, instilled in me strong ethics and values, and a desire for justice. They also filled me with inspiration to never give up and keep building the scaffolding to climb higher, not just for me, but for those who come after me.

My husband, Wes Robb, and son, Owen Robb, daily provide the love and support that keeps me going through good times and bad. Their encouragement, patience, wisdom, and sheer goofiness are truly the secret to my success and happiness.

With their support, I have lost the weight, and I will finally be able to have my much-needed knee replacement surgeries. I have no doubt that with their constant support and my brand-new knees, I will be able to continue climbing (figuratively and literally) to reach all of my dreams!

Jackie Robb is the co-owner of R&R Environmental Partners LLC, a multifaceted environmental, health, and safety consulting firm providing EHS experts as problem solving partners. She holds a B.S. in Mining Engineering from Missouri University of Science & Technology, and has more than thirty years of consulting experience in the St. Louis, Missouri area, as well as nine additional states. She is a proud member of Kindred UCC in Maplewood, Missouri, and is a strong social justice advocate and LGBTQIA+ ally.

Jackie is obsessed with everything about real estate, history, especially the Industrial Revolution, genealogy, musicals, and all things Disney.

In her free time, she plays World of Warcraft with her hubby, FaceTimes with her son at college, watches Great Courses and British TV shows, visits with friends/family, including her beloved "Tribe," and plays puzzle games. Jackie loves to plan trips and travel, and photograph everything! She is looking forward to getting out on her bike with her new knees!

Please scan the QR code to connect with this author.

G.R.I.T.

Mike Tallis

Building a Legacy

Making money was something that I've thought about for as long as I can remember. At five years old, I would color pictures, thinking they were so good that I could sell them for $5 each on the neighborhood corner. During the summer, I would set up a lemonade stand, and I also sold bubble gum in front of the pool before enjoying the pool with my friends. During junior high, I would have my mom take me to the five-and-dime store so I could load up on candy to sell them for twenty-five cents each. No matter what I was doing, I was always finding ways to make money.

Fast forward to college. I was playing baseball on a scholarship; life dealt me a hand that forced me to make a life-changing decision. My father was diagnosed with cancer and only given a short time to live. I made the decision to stop playing baseball and move back home to help take care of my family; it was time for me to think about my career and what I wanted to do, since the dream of making it to the pros was no longer in the cards for me. I discovered that I really enjoyed building relationships through problem-solving. Given my athletic background, fitness was always a priority. So, I got certified to be a personal trainer at the age of nineteen. By age twenty-one, I took a leap of faith and opened my first brick-and-mortar business—a personal training service.

Thinking back on my childhood entrepreneurial endeavors, I had taken tremendous pride in everything I did, and I believed in myself. Now it was time to show consistent hard work with sacrifice while continuing to sharpen my people-building skills. During my twenty-plus years in the fitness industry, I was honored to teach a positive lifestyle while also building a great business. Some of the achievements included being named a Top 30 Under 30 honoree in the *St. Louis Small Business Journal* for three years in a row, being featured in the Fast Forward section of the *St. Louis Business Journal,* and being named as one of the nation's Top 100 Personal Trainers.

When the global pandemic struck in 2020, fitness was labeled as non-essential, and my gym was closed for three months. I am a firm believer in finding the silver lining in all things that seem negative, because I know that everything is for my good. At that time, I was forty years old with three kids. I knew I needed to pivot and start a business that was deemed essential. After a few months looking for a gap that needed to be filled, I had a conversation in which I instantly saw the opportunity, and I walked through the door.

Cherokee Hauling was formed in 2021 with the sole purpose of honoring my family's Native American roots and leaving a legacy. I am a citizen of the Cherokee Nation, where many of my ancestors and current family members live on the reservations in Tahlequah, Oklahoma. My family roots have been traced back to 1807, where my fourth great-grandfather, Wi Waw SeTy and his wife, Na' Ke, lived in North Carolina, along with their two sons. Like many, they were forced to head west on the Trail of Tears in 1838. While in a holding camp prior to the 838-mile journey to Oklahoma, Wi Waw Se Ty, Na' Ke, and their oldest son died of dysentery. The youngest son, Tonniette, at the age of three, was the lone survivor. One of the families along the trail raised and cared for Tonniette when they arrived in Oklahoma. In 1861, Tonniette served in the

American Civil War for the Confederate Army, and by 1872, Tonniette had a son named Levi. Levi would be my second great-grandfather and the last full-blooded Native American in the family's bloodline.

I got the opportunity to take my family to Tahlequah, Oklahoma, last year for the big holiday pow-wow. While there, we sat down with my oldest living relative—who still teaches Cherokee at the community college—to learn more about our family's heritage. I came to learn that the Ketcher community was forced to shut down during the Great Depression, and the land was bought by the government for eight cents per acre, after which most of my family had settled into comfort, adopting the mentality of living to work rather than working to live. The Ketcher community was filled with love for the people and community. They offered to lease their land to those who did not get any land so they could build a home and settle with their families. The community also included a school, a lumber mill, a post office, and a courthouse. All I could think about when I read about the Ketcher community—and later learned more detailed stories from my relative, Sammy Ketcher—is how much of a positive impact they had on so many people. This truly was an act of the heart and forward-thinking for their time and culture. This was the moment I decided that Cherokee Hauling was going to be more than a dump truck business. Cherokee Hauling was going to make an impact within the construction community by leading the way for positive change in eastern Missouri. This will be my legacy—one that I hope my kids will one day pick up and carry forward.

So, how does one just start over with a new business in a completely different industry? That is a tough task. When you throw in the variables of being forty years old with three kids and all the responsibilities and commitments of life, the fear of the unknown can be crippling and often will cause complacency. I had to have the perspective that there was no turning back—that forward was the only option! I chose to put my faith in God, and I trusted that I can't be blessed with something new if I continue to be comfortable with something old. I decided to use my twenty-plus years of relationship-building skills by focusing my time on simply being a solution to other people's problems. Was it scary to start over in a whole new industry where I really didn't know how the game was played? Yes! However, the excitement of learning something new and building something with my twenty-plus years of entrepreneurial experience superseded the fear. I quickly sought out the different associations in the area that related to construction, and I felt at home with SITE Improvement Association. I started volunteering my time at the annual golf tournament and attended every event they held. I joined one of the committees and, after a couple of years, ran for the Board of Directors. Today I am a board member, chair a committee, and sit on two others. The friends and trusted partners I have gained have become invaluable.

Cherokee Hauling started with one dump truck, and I spent the first year learning the industry and working on the certification process for my Minority Business Enterprise (MBE) and Disadvantaged Business Enterprise (DBE). We ended the first year in the black, which was a win with all the startup costs of a new business. By the second quarter of year two, Cherokee bought its second truck. We also received our DBE certification in the second quarter, which opened the opportunity for us to gain our first regular customer. Now, having the capability of keeping both dump trucks busy daily, we were in a position by the third quarter to buy a third truck.

Cherokee experienced 164 percent growth in the second year, and we also received our MBE certification. This certification would again narrow the funnel of competition, offering Cherokee the opportunity to showcase our high standards for customer service. Everything was positioning itself for the building of a strong business foundation. I only paid myself when I drove—and at the same rate I paid my drivers. Everything else went back into the business to build our working capital. In year three of the business, Cherokee really started picking up momentum. Cherokee Hauling's brand was beginning to gain recognition, with a few trucks on the road daily, and my continued focus on building relationships and developing business. We started bidding on projects with new companies, winning contracts for the first time. In order to push our revenue forward a bit faster, we expanded our services by adding night work to our schedule. This was also a way to lower our per-unit cost for recurring expenses, like insurance and truck payments.

Year three was definitely a year where I knew I needed to expand my hours by leading the nights. I ran the front office during the day and drove a truck every night doing major road repairs for Missouri Department of Transportation (MoDOT) projects. This push allowed Cherokee to buy truck number four. We were able to buy a newer used truck—also our first automatic. The newer trucks certainly cut down on some of the major maintenance repairs. Ending year three, Cherokee Hauling was named MOKAN's 2023 Emerging Business of the Year. We added a fifth dump truck and grew another 275 percent.

Entering year four, we had five of our own trucks and began adding hired haulers to our network to better serve our customers' needs. By the end of the first quarter, we were averaging fifteen trucks a day out on job sites. As we entered the summer, the momentum of our hired hauler network became contagious, as we continued to add multiple trucks to our network daily. Entering the fall, Cherokee Hauling was putting around seventy-five trucks a day out on jobs. We also added a couple more new trucks to our own fleet, increasing our fleet to seven dump trucks. Cherokee continued to see triple-digit growth, growing another 220 percent.

Now, all these wins sound great, and that is how I choose to look at the big picture. Because if I were to share the day-to-day battles and all the hurdles that Cherokee has had to overcome, it wouldn't be very glamorous or seem so easy. Why? Because it's not. Business is tough. Life is hard. It takes someone who can endure all the challenges and solve problems quickly. I have been asked many times throughout my life about the recipe for success. There are many things I would say that would give you similar results, but you must first figure out what success is. What is success to you? Find your purpose first, then create a plan of action on how you want to get there.

No one would drive from New York to Los Angeles without knowing what roads they were going to take. The same is true in life and in business. Know what you want, set goals, and execute those goals with an action plan. It all comes down to one word: consistency! Be willing to believe in yourself. Have the discipline to get up every day ready to go to battle and deal with what life throws at you. Know that some days you will lose—whether that be the business losing money that day or taking a step backwards by losing a key employee. Some days are tough, but with grit and a focus on the big picture, you can win the week. Win four out of seven days, and I promise your business will trend in the right direction over the course of a month, a quarter, and even a year.

As I wrap up my story, I hope that you found it relatable and inspiring. I believe that if I can grab one gold nugget from something I read and apply it to my life, then it was worth reading. Go win the day!

Mike Tallis is the managing owner of Cherokee Hauling, LLC, a leading provider of hauling services in the St. Louis market. With over twenty-five years of experience in the customer service industry, Mike has developed a strong focus on building relationships. Mike's passion for helping others and solving problems is reflected in his commitment to delivering the highest level of customer service.

In addition to his professional success, Mike is a three-time Hall of Famer at various levels of baseball and has earned bodybuilding titles in Missouri and Arkansas. His dedication to personal excellence is matched by his involvement in industry leadership. As a board member of the SITE Improvement Association, Mike sits on several committees and chairs the Inclusion Task Force.

Mike's combination of business acumen, community involvement, and personal achievement makes him a well-rounded leader, committed to the growth of his company and the betterment of the industry.

G.R.I.T.

Jennifer Ayeni

Farm Family Values
Build Strong Business

When you first meet me, you might first notice my sweet, warm demeanor, but underneath that welcoming glow is a story built by grit, hustle, and a deep desire to serve others. I'm Jennifer Ayeni, the franchise owner of Fizz Facial Bar in St. Louis, Missouri, and my journey into entrepreneurship has been anything but ordinary. It's been shaped by rural upbringing, a passion for service, breaking barriers, and a leap of faith into an industry where Fizz Facial Bar is redefining the spa experience.

My story begins on a farm in rural southern Missouri, before later moving to the Appalachian mountains of Eastern Kentucky. The rhythms of farm life and watching my father's tireless work ethic shaped my character. Weekends meant hauling wood, building fences, or whatever my dad had lined up for us. While I often begged to stay inside and play school, I still got the job done—reluctantly at times. I remember waking up early before school to bottle-feed baby calves. My dad would remove the calves from their moms to give me a chore with purpose—to teach me responsibility and show me that someone (or something) was counting on me to follow through to survive.

From those early years, I learned that hard work builds character, never to give up, there's more than one way to solve a problem, and you can always find a way to make it work if you're willing to work at it.

Although I knew early on that farm life wasn't my calling, earning my first paycheck in seventh grade—detasseling corn for minimum wage—was a defining moment. I remember cashing that check entirely in one-dollar bills just to feel the weight of my work. That moment sparked something inside me. I knew then that while I might leave the farm, I'd carry that work ethic into whatever I chose to do.

I went on to attend Morehead State University in Eastern Kentucky and pursued a career in radio and television journalism. I reported, anchored, and produced the news at WMKY Public Radio, WKAG in Hopkinsville, Kentucky, and WSAZ in Huntington and Charleston, West Virginia.

But when I became a mother, I knew that career wouldn't support the life I wanted to create for my family. I wanted to be the kind of mom I had—present and involved. Still, I couldn't sit idly for long. When my son turned one, I went back to college part-time to pursue a master's degree in education and earned my teaching degree.

I became the first in my family—on both sides—to earn a master's degree. It empowered me to make a difference not only in my son's life but in the lives of many other children who needed an advocate in their lives too. A few years later, I earned a second master's degree in K-12 school counseling and served in public education for nearly 15 years. Then, I found myself entering a new chapter.

As our children approached their final years of high school, my husband asked me a question that I hadn't thought about in years and years. He asked me, "If you could do anything, what would it be?" Wow, I could not answer the question. I planned what I was doing around what I wanted my family to have. He reminded me we would be empty nesters soon, and there is a world of opportunities. At the same time, I was struggling with some of my own skin issues and seeing a dermatologist.

I stumbled across a friend's post on social media about Fizz Facial Bar. A few of my teacher friends had gone after work for facials together. Intrigued, I searched for anything like it in the St. Louis, Missouri region and found nothing. I shared my excitement with my husband, Ola Ayeni, a serial entrepreneur, and he encouraged me to reach out to the founder and owner herself. When I did and didn't hear anything, my husband told me to reach out again. Thank goodness for the question my husband asked me, his continued encouragement to dream again, and his guidance to seek what God has in store for me in the next season of life. That's when I finally connected with Crystal Booth, the founder, esthetician, and creative director of Fizz Facial Bar

I was overjoyed. I told Crystal, "I absolutely love this concept you created, and we have to find a way to bring Fizz Facial Bar to St. Louis, Missouri—but first, my husband and I need to come get facials!"

After experiencing the facials in a friendly, unique salon setup, and learning more about the concept, we traveled the country to try out other facial bars—and none compared to Fizz Facial Bar! The upbeat vibe, the selection of medical-grade skincare lines that worked for both me and my husband, and the way estheticians empowered and educated clients—it was everything I had been looking for. Fizz Facial Bar was it!

Fizz Facial Bar is not your typical spa, and I'm not your typical spa franchise owner. I have poured myself into this business and am there on nearly a daily basis. Fizz Facial Bar breaks all the traditional rules. It's an open-concept skincare studio that's welcoming and upbeat. You can sit at the bar and get facials with a friend! "Our company's motto is, 'No Fuss, Just Fizz,' meaning we 'cut out time wasters and money wasters' to make skincare more affordable and accessible for everyone," I often share with others.

There was a gap in the skincare market—something that wasn't intimidating, uptight, or exclusive. Fizz Facial Bar offered something radically different. Our treatments take just 30 minutes, making skincare approachable for even the busiest clients. If you have a face, you need a facial!

Fizz Facial Bar is more than skincare. It's about connection. I know people can connect over facials because that's how I've made lifelong friends. I remember begging my mom to let me have a sleepover in seventh grade to meet new friends after changing schools. I even found a DIY strawberry yogurt facial recipe in *Teen Magazine* and made it for the party. I'm still friends with those girls today.

When I brought Fizz Facial Bar to St. Louis, Missouri, I wanted to create that same kind of space, so I added the "bubble lounge," a party area perfect for birthdays, girls' nights, and wellness events.

I find purpose in the small moments—a client regaining confidence, a mother and daughter bonding, or a friend group laughing at the facial bar. It warms my heart and brings a smile to my face.

Looking back, I credit my success to three things: faith, boldness, and surrounding myself with the right people. My advice to aspiring entrepreneurs? Take the next step of faith. You don't need the entire road map—just enough to move forward. Over-analyzing can paralyze you. Start now. I relied on prayer, God opening the right doors and closing the wrong ones. I mean, who was I? I'm not a business owner, I had no experience in skin care. I was a teacher and school counselor, but God showed me to give Him what I've got, and He will turn it into a lot! That's what God has done and continues to do in and through me!

With the lack of business knowledge, my husband complimented me well, but running a business is hard work! No one works harder at hustling than a business owner. This new facial bar concept is something that people have to be educated on and buy into. Yes, we are fun, but we offer effective, targeted, results-driven services while not compromising on medical-grade products, ingredients, licensed estheticians, and sought-after services. With anything new, you have to find creative ways to get potential clients into your door and keep them! The best way to receive is to give! That's what we did! We gave people the opportunity to come in and experience a facial, provide us feedback, and from that, we learn and continue to grow!

Community matters deeply to me. I believe in surrounding myself with like-minded, make-it-happen people. I protect my energy, invite creativity, and stay flexible enough to pivot when needed.

Giving back is part of my mission. At Fizz Facial Bar, we create fundraising opportunities for nonprofits. I don't just want Fizz Facial Bar to succeed as a business. I want it to be a platform that empowers everyone to build confidence and know their worth.

At the heart of everything I do is one thing: truly getting to know our clients. Fizz Facial Bar welcomes all types of clients—from those wanting to relax to those with specific skincare concerns. Our licensed estheticians work one-on-one with clients to create customized routines.

Fizz Facial Bar also attracts people who have felt out of place in traditional spas. Our approachable, no-pressure vibe makes clients feel at home. We listen carefully, adapt our services to meet real needs, and always put people first. I strive to leave our clients and staff better than we found them.

What truly sets me apart is my vision. Fizz Facial Bar is more than a business—it's a reflection of my values, my personality, and my faith. I'm intentional about joy. I want everyone who walks through our doors, clients or staff, to feel valued, seen, and loved.

From feeding calves before sunrise to bringing a new kind of spa experience to St. Louis, Missouri—my journey is proof that grit and grace can coexist.

I'm still dreaming big. I'm committed to growing Fizz Facial Bar into more communities across the St. Louis, Missouri region and into other communities. I believe in faith, community, perseverance, and a little sparkle—and I know that with the right care, we are breaking barriers and shaking up the skin care market.

Jennifer Ayeni is the franchise owner of Fizz Facial Bar in St. Louis, Missouri. Her journey into entrepreneurship has been shaped by grit, faith, and a passion for serving others. With degrees in journalism, education, and counseling, she spent nearly 15 years in public education before discovering Fizz Facial Bar, a skincare studio that felt radically different. Jennifer knew instantly that she had to find a way to bring it to her community. Fizz Facial Bar isn't just a business—it's a reflection of her values, energy, and heart.

Jennifer was selected as a participant in the first Coro Women Leadership in STEM in St. Louis, Missouri. She is involved in the Rooted Sisters Christian business women organization, the Chesterfield, Missouri Chamber, Babes in Business, and is a supporter of the African Chamber and the International Institute. She loves building community through collaboration and giving back. Jennifer enjoys spending time traveling the world with her husband and surrounding herself with family (four children), extended family, and friends!

Please scan the QR code to connect with this author.

G.R.I.T.

Maureen Daley

The Foundation of Grit: Resilience to Daley Design

I can remember my parents always working. Their work ethic helped shape me into who I am today. The mantra was: If you want something, then work for it. And work for it, they did. I was always humbled by my father's ability to log in long hours in extreme conditions. He was a union pipe coverer, working in sweltering attics and crawlspaces while wearing a turtle neck to protect his skin from particulates and fiberglass insulation. Getting up as early as 3 a.m. to beat the heat, he often put in a full day's work before most people started theirs. My mother worked nights in the service industry, sacrificing weekends and sometimes holidays to ensure our family was taken care of. I learned through their drive and sacrifice what it meant to work hard and dedicate yourself to the task at hand. They taught me to take pride in everything I do.

As a young girl, I was diagnosed with dyslexia. At the time, I didn't fully understand the diagnosis, but soon realized it meant I had to learn differently than others and work twice as hard as my contemporaries to keep up. While difficult, I didn't let it deter me from learning and growing daily.

Liz, my sister, is a reading specialist and works with students who have dyslexia. She shares new findings and tips about dyslexia that I adopt and use each day.

I have always been impressed and inspired by those who grapple with problems and continue to learn their way through them, using each one as a moment of growth.

While I have always been drawn to art, it wasn't until I studied at Webster University that my love for design and all it could provide took root. I had a fantastic professor named Noriko Yuasa, who instilled a sense of possibility within design. Calling all of us her "design babies," she took the time to nurture my creativity and helped me grow as an artist, a designer, and as a person. She checks in on all her students now and then, even today.

After I completed an internship with a local design agency in St. Louis, Missouri, they offered me a job. I took it immediately. Excited to begin my career, I worked with mid-to-large clients, most with their own in-house marketing and design teams. I was a sponge in those early days, absorbing all the tips and suggestions from a strong mentorship. I began to find myself, know my strengths and weaknesses, and learn what it took to be a successful designer.

I made an impression on my boss, who fed my desire to learn and helped shape my early career. When the 2008 recession hit, it hit hard. The marketing budget was significantly slashed, and I watched as my friends and fellow employees were let go one by one.

When the dust cleared, it was just my boss and me remaining. While it felt good to be thought of so highly, I was terrified. It was a scary time in my life. I had just gotten married and bought a house. I had expenses that I'd never had before.

Were we going to lose our house? Would we have to give up that dream?

There were many nights when my husband and I talked about our future and what we wanted for our future. It helped me realize the possibilities and opportunities lying ahead of me. The question was, would I be brave enough to take the leap?

As it turned out, Daley Design was founded in 2009 as a way to turn passion into purpose.

The leap was a catalyst for me to consider what type of clients I wanted to serve. I was in charge. My decisions. My choices. They all impacted the kind of business I would build. By working with large companies in my first job, I realized there was an entire untapped world of small-to-medium businesses that typically couldn't afford traditional design agencies. They still needed help and support, but they simply didn't have the capital. Pouring their blood, sweat, and tears into building something from nothing made me want to help them take the next step.

I've always been fascinated by watching small business clients evolve and grow into something more, into something unimagined. Realizing our design work played a part in that journey is so fulfilling and so humbling. I enjoy forming partnerships with my clients, lasting relationships that grow with their continued success. Whether it's creating a brand identity, a website, or a print piece, providing something with a lasting impact on a business's success never gets old.

There's a reason the old business adage states: new companies won't see profits in the first few years. It's because it's the truth. They aren't wrong. Trying to launch my business during a recession was not an easy task. The only good thing was that I had incredibly low overhead. My basic startup cost was for software and a new computer. My biggest asset? My work ethic.

I was relentless in pursuing my dream, in making my business a success. I realized the small-to-medium-sized businesses were the same as mine. They were putting everything they had into being a success. They just needed a little help. And I was just the help they needed.

The reality of running my own business hit me pretty hard. I did everything for the business: marketing, sales, proposals, purchasing, and bookkeeping. Was it exhausting? Yes. Would I have changed it for the world? Never.

I started off slow, networking with groups and local businesses, honing my sales skills and my business acumen along the way. Many of those relationships I built in 2009 are still part of my network today.

When my husband joined the ranks, I was able to take a few of those hats off. With degrees in diplomacy and foreign affairs, he pivoted with me and taught himself web development. Tackling CSS, WordPress, and HTML, he expanded the services we could provide. I was impressed with his fortitude and am so proud of the grit he displayed. Working with my husband as a true partner in the business has been so rewarding. Supporting each other, we've grown by leaps and bounds, and the trust in ourselves grows each day.

Watching the pandemic coverage and seeing it spread worldwide was terrifying. I panicked. In 2020, the world was handed a new reality. I had no idea what it might mean for my business or my clients. Staying small helped us transition to the new world. We had amazing clients, great referrals, and low costs. It helped us to build a network of partners, clients, and vendors who not only challenge us but also inspire us.

While our bread and butter is clearly branding and website design, I am always seeking new revenue streams and new ways of helping our clients get more return on their designs.

My motto has always been: Design should work for you.

When I work with a business, I'm not seeking a solution for today, but a solution for the future. Consider Coca-Cola®, a brand we all know. It's been around since the late 1800s. And while they have evolved over time, the core design principles of logo and marketing haven't. That is the true power of intentional branding. When done right, it can become timeless, recognizable, and provide continued effectiveness year after year.

When I consider where I've come from and how many miles my journey has taken me, I take stock in my successes, shortcomings, and challenges. But I don't do that for long. I am continually hungry for the next success story, the next challenge, and the next step in my personal and professional growth. I want to continue meeting new people, mastering new skills, and building confidence.

That's where true grit comes to roost. In the possibility. In the knowledge that I'm doing the work, again and again, with intention and every ounce of my heart.

If I could offer any advice to my fellow entrepreneurs, it is this: surround yourself with those who support you and your cause. In the simplest of terms, having someone say, "You've got this," when the chips are down makes all the difference. Emotional encouragement and practical guidance from diverse perspectives are invaluable. The robust support system reduces stress and enhances resilience to tackle anything.

Success is right around the corner.

Reach for it!

Maureen Daley is the owner and creative director of Daley Design. Offering more than 20 years of design experience, she helps her clients with their branding and marketing approach.

Graduating from Webster University's art program, Maureen was inspired by her hardworking parents and small business owners. Starting her business during the 2008 recession wasn't easy, but her determination helped her build it into an international success.

Maureen's collaborative approach has received worldwide recognition. She frequently works with companies that are often ignored by traditional agencies. Her specialties include web design and branding, while utilizing both digital and print solutions.

Finding inspiration from other travelers, Maureen is a student of life, gaining knowledge from other cultures and viewpoints, culminating in her mindset: design is about impact and providing work that will stand the test of time. In her free time, she enjoys golf and spending time with her family.

Please scan the QR code to connect with this author.

G.R.I.T.

Bill Donovan

Take the Leap

Long before Rockwood Litho officially launched, I was a college graduate trying to find my place in the world. I realized sales was a good fit for me—I wanted to be face-to-face with the customer, listen to what they need, form a relationship, and help them succeed. I responded to a LinkedIn job posting and ended up landing a commercial print sales job. The overall sentiment was that "ink on paper" and the print industry was not booming. However, I found success, partly because I was a younger sales rep and brought new energy, while most of my co-workers had been in their careers for decades. I was young and coachable.

I followed a process to prospect for new customers that I still use today. I prepared a ton of boxes with marketing items (notepad, pen, promo item, and a few samples) and kept them in my car. I made a route based on an old-school map-routing program and mapped out multiple stops to maximize my time. A coworker suggested that I start traveling outside of the St. Louis area to do overnight trips. This hadn't been done before at the company, but I approached my boss with a plan. They had confidence that I would be able to grow my sales quicker with this strategy. In my time there, I brought in over one hundred new customers, continually growing my sales year after year. I was on pace to continue that growth, but I decided to take my sales experience to a national level and see if my success would translate to a different industry—banking software. I jumped into this new role. I started traveling, learning new skills, and meeting new people. It was an adjustment—daily virtual meetings and wearing a suit and tie every day. This job had its perks, but I quickly realized that it wasn't what I was meant to do.

I first had the idea to launch my own company long before I left the printing industry. However, that's all it was—an idea. I wasn't sure that it was something I could do. My wife and I wanted to grow our family and move into a new home, and it was hard to imagine leaving the security of a salary and solid insurance plan to take that leap. So, it sat on the back burner. I was accustomed to taking direction and training from management, but I really wanted to be my own boss and set my own schedule. I also had several people in my life who had launched their own companies, proving that if you stay focused and determined, you can be successful.

As the urge grew, I knew I wanted to get serious about getting started, but I also knew that I had to do it at my own pace. Once I realized that I wanted to make it official, I searched for the perfect name. The list of name ideas was colorful—looking back now, I laugh. We definitely landed on the right name. Since we live in the Rockwood School District, I wanted that to be represented in the name. I also wanted the name to be connected to my roots and why I fell in love with the industry in the first place. Litho is an old-school printing term, but coincidentally, it has very little to do with our business. But it sounds really cool, right? While looking out the back window of our new home that we had just built, I snapped a picture of a tree. I sent it to a friend who freelanced in graphic design and asked her to pair CMYK printing colors with the tree. She worked her magic, and our logo was born.

My biggest challenge was building a completely new customer base. I had to step out of my comfort zone of ink-on-paper to explore promotional products and apparel. The game changer was joining a supplier network that enabled us to offer thousands of items with competitive pricing. At our first promo trade show, we really started to understand how far we could take this business. There were hundreds of vendors offering thousands of items, and we had barely scratched the surface. It was like trick-or-treating for business owners. Our wheels started turning. The other challenge I faced was time management. It was difficult to focus on my growing company while still giving my time and energy to my full-time, salaried job. I knew I needed to prioritize Rockwood Litho if I wanted it to grow, but I struggled daily to make that happen. This was life for five years. During this time, my wife and I had two more kids, she had some big career changes, and I started coaching two softball teams. We were juggling a lot. Family time is important, and I could feel myself stretching thin.

My wife, Lori, was at a crossroads in her career, and we decided that if she put her focus on our company, I could stay in my current job longer. So that's what we did. While sitting in a local coffee shop one morning, we took our first leap and bought an embroidery machine and a heat press. Until then, we had been outsourcing *everything*. This was a big deal for us to take some of the production in-house to increase profits and deliver orders quicker. We had no idea what we were doing. We didn't know what machines we needed, and we had no idea how to operate anything. We were naive. We initially bought a $500 sewing/embroidery machine and quickly realized that it was not enough to handle the business we wanted to bring in. So, we upgraded to a much more expensive commercial-grade machine. This thing was a beast—an intimidating machine, to say the least. After a lot (and I mean *a lot*) of trial and error, we figured it out.

We wanted to bring Direct-to-Film (DTF) printing in-house. We had spent thousands of dollars outsourcing our custom apparel, and we knew that we wanted this to be a main focus of our company, so we needed to figure out how to bring this in-house as well. We bought a desktop printer that we thought would be the answer to our problems. It was not. It was a mess and has been one of the biggest learning lessons to date for us. We didn't do enough research and didn't fully understand the process. It wasn't even DTF technology; it was toner-based. It took seven minutes to make one shirt, and we needed a much quicker process. It was an eye-opening experience. We ended up returning that printer as well and really had to take a step back and realize that we needed to slow down and really do our homework.

Our next purchase would be our biggest. We had countless conversations about which DTF printer to buy. If we took this step, that was it. We were undoubtedly and completely bought in. I knew that's what I wanted to do; Lori took a little more convincing. We ultimately decided it was time and bought our first DTF printer. This thing was five feet wide and massive. Somehow, we had to move it down our basement stairs. Nothing was going to stop us from getting it down to our basement, though, and I even had to remove the door and trim. Soon after the printer was delivered, we bought our first dual heat press. I built a room in our basement that became our print shop, and just like that, we were a fully functioning, in-house printing company. It felt like we were moving in the right direction, and we had finally found our groove. The problem was, I was still dividing my time between Rockwood Litho and my salary job.

It was obvious that the more attention and energy I put into Rockwood Litho, the more success we experienced. It sounds so simple. But leaving the safety net of a salaried position was tougher than ever with the responsibilities of having three small kids. Business was growing quickly; Lori was running the day-to-day, and it was time for me to fully embrace being a business owner and let go of the safety net. I needed to give Rockwood Litho my undivided attention, and I knew that once I did that, there would be no looking back.

We weren't fully prepared for the bonding that comes with running a company full-time as a husband and wife. While I was working my salaried job, I was traveling and sitting in on work meetings. We had days when we never saw each other. That ended. We were dependent on each other, and the success of our company landed on both of us now. We cannot successfully run this company without complete transparency and communication. It is hard to separate "business" and "family" when the business is being run under the same roof that we're raising our three kids in. It's nearly impossible to detach yourself from one thing to focus on another. We're constantly working on finding a balance. But ultimately, we have discovered that we are way more effective together, and we are intentional about how we spend our time with each other and our kids.

Time management, or lack of time, is my greatest challenge in growing the business. Prioritizing what gets done each day is a struggle—I got behind on sending invoices, and cash flow became a real issue. This is absolutely the most critical aspect of any healthy and successful business. Without money coming in, you can't survive. I spent many days and nights catching up and have since found a better way to manage cash flow.

Another challenge became apparent. Between machines, supplies, blank apparel items, and orders, we quickly outgrew the space in our home, and it was starting to take over the rest of the house. So, the hunt for a commercial space began. We didn't need much—just 1200+ square feet, and we were excited to find a new home for the company. It's been a rollercoaster. Finding something that made sense financially but also logistically was difficult. We looked at properties and ran into every roadblock you can imagine. Everything commercial was either too small, or too big, or too expensive. We were struggling to find our place while Rockwood Litho was still consistently growing. We needed help, but didn't want to hire anyone while we were still operating out of our home, so we felt like we were racing against time. Until we found our new space for Rockwood Litho, we continued operating out of our home. It wasn't ideal, but it worked.

That brings us to today. In the first five years of the company, we sent out under four hundred invoices. That's more than doubled in the last ten months. We've added over thirty custom online stores and bought two more dual-heat presses. Our customer base has more than quadrupled and is expanding more than we imagined. We've joined networking groups and sponsored events, schools, and teams. We have big plans to expand our capabilities and capacity. We recently found a commercial space that is close to home, has plenty of space for future expansion, and checks all the boxes. The lease is signed, and once we are settled in, we plan to buy more printers and hire people. We may even add traditional screen printing. The possibilities are endless. We are constantly learning and evolving as a small business—and as people. Our foundation as a husband-wife duo is one of our greatest selling points. The connections we've made with our customers are priceless, because they know the values we stand on and the product we deliver. The company is thriving, and we are excited to see what develops in the coming years. My advice to anyone wanting to start a new business…take the leap!

Bill Donovan, MBA, is an independent author featured in the book *Successful Entrepreneurs with G.R.I.T.* He owns and operates Rockwood Litho, based in Eureka, Missouri, which creates custom print, promo, and apparel for its customers. Bill has earned degrees in business from Fontbonne University and Lindenwood University. Bill is passionate about networking, creating new things, spending time with family, coaching youth softball, golfing, watching professional sports, and traveling.

Please scan the QR code to connect with this author.

G.R.I.T.

Rolanda Finch

How Loving My Birthday Sparked a Mission

My birthday is September 14. This is my favorite day of the year!

I actually love celebrating my birthday the entire month of September. As a child, my family made sure each birthday was special. I vividly remember my 9th birthday—the yellow homemade special dress (I've always been tall, so my mom made most of my clothes), the yummy treats, and the friends and family celebrating me.

Fast forward thirty-nine years. In my full-time job, I was teaching leaders in a Fortune Global 500 how to leave their legacy. It occurred to me: *"What will be my legacy?"* By choice, I did not have children. I thought, *"How will people remember me? Will I just be 'the late employee of x company?'"* I did not want that for myself. I knew there had to be more that I wanted people to remember about me.

I frequently volunteered at a homeless shelter as part of my former church's outreach. While visiting one of the shelters, I noticed there were a lot of children running around, just being children. One day, sadness came over me as I thought, "How will these children remember their birthday? Like me, will the little girl have a vivid memory of her birthday? Will she have the memory of being unable to celebrate because she and her family were in a shelter?" Asking a child to understand that was too much.

This is when I had my a-ha moment. I knew I had to change birthday memories for these kiddos.

I asked the executive director if I could give monthly birthday parties for their children. I would come in as Rolanda, no organization, and give all children in the shelter a birthday party. Everyone at the shelter could attend, and the birthday children would be treated extra special. After all, it was their special month. He agreed. Soon, people wanted to know how they could get involved and if I was a 501(c)(3) nonprofit. I was not. I had no idea that I needed to be one. After all, this was a passion project, not a business. I had a job. After numerous requests, I decided to move forward with making it a nonprofit business. But not before I exercised my corporate mindset to pilot other shelters to ensure this was a good idea. I selected a domestic violence shelter. My thought was that these children are in hiding. Mom is scared and in survival mode; unfortunately, birthdays will be forgotten. Like the homeless shelters, there were no resources (people and funds) to celebrate birthdays.

The homeless and domestic violence shelters loved the idea, and It's Your Birthday, Inc. (IYBI) was born, and I became "The Birthday Lady!"— a name affectionately given by a birthday kiddo.

When I began IYBI, our only option was a birthday party for kiddos five to twelve years old, thinking that under five, they would not remember, and over twelve, they are teens who would not care about a party. Very quickly, the shelters shared with us how siblings were sad when they were not celebrated because we would celebrate a six-year-old girl and not her three-year-old brother. This was a quick lesson learned and required a change in our mission to celebrate all children and youth in the shelters we serve. Currently, one of our shelters is for youth 16-22. Proving, everyone wants to be celebrated on their special day with cake and ice cream!

After a year of hosting birthday parties where we decorated the space with colorful balloons and cheerful birthday banners, we also provided entertaining activities such as balloon artists, magicians, science experiments, cupcake challenges, and "minute-to-win-it" games for the kiddos. Additionally, we offered delicious treats and toys for all of the children. For the mommies who attended the party, we included beauty products and hygiene items.

To differentiate ourselves from other organizations, IYBI added four additional birthday choices. Including the Birthday Party, we now have a total of five birthday options.

One is a Birthday-in-a-Box. This is a plain brown cardboard box decorated by volunteers, filled with toys for younger kiddos, fast-food gift cards, and hygiene products for youth. The box also contains a Schnucks gift card for the mom to purchase the themed birthday cake—after all, unless your mom is a professional baker, no one wants their mom to try to bake a Spider-Man birthday cake. Also, mom does not need the stress. It's Your Birthday, Inc. will never put our logo on the box, allowing the mom to gift the box to her child.

Another option is a Birthday Surprise that allows the mom to select an online gift, send IYBI the link, and we place the order and send the gift to the shelter for the mom to give to their birthday kiddo. It's Your Birthday, Inc. will also have it gift wrapped, if requested. Besides ensuring the kiddos enjoy their special day, it is important for IYBI to be a comfort to the moms during this difficult time. We want the kiddo to say, "Thanks, Mom."

It's Your Birthday, Inc. created a Birthday-in-a-Class option when we learned how kiddos in shelters didn't feel "normal" when their classmates were celebrated, and they were not on their special day. It's Your Birthday, Inc. works with the school to create a birthday experience for the kiddo and their classmates to enjoy. IYBI delivers cupcakes and a birthday gift to the class and tells the child, "Your mom sent us." If requested, we will also host a themed classroom party.

Lastly, in 2021, the Happy Born Day option was created at the suggestion of one of our shelter partners. Moms who give birth while in the shelter are able to order a gift for their newborn or themselves. This gift can give the new mom a sense of self-worth during this challenging time.

With all our birthday options, we give the young birthday child a Happy Birthday Teddy Bear.

During the early days, we provided decorations in the Birthday-in-a-Box along with toys for moms who wanted to give their kiddo a party. With one of our short-term shelters, we would have boxes on hand in case of a "birthday emergency." Yes, they exist.

I remember receiving a call from a shelter that had a mom come in during the night with a daughter whose fifth birthday was in a couple of days. Imagine the child's disappointment as she thinks because they are now in this strange place with other children she has never met. The child thinks, "Surely, Mom will not remember my birthday." To her surprise, Mom was excited to learn the shelter had an IYBI Birthday-in-a-Box with toys and supplies to ensure her daughter had a fun princess party as she navigated keeping them safe from her abuser. With It's Your Birthday, Inc.'s help, a better birthday memory was created for this little five-year-old girl.

Since I started IYBI, I have always worked a full-time job. Now, I was also a full-time entrepreneur: a nonprofit founder and chief birthday officer. This multi-role came with many responsibilities, challenges, and rewards. I recall many times being in a hotel room (for my full-time job) with a seven-hour time difference, planning a party we would host when I returned, or running to a party store during a lunch break because there was a "birthday emergency."

One of my biggest challenges is remembering to stay true to our mission: *To create fun and memorable birthday experiences for children in homeless and domestic violence shelters.* Throughout the years, It's Your Birthday, Inc. received many opportunities for financial gains if we offered our services to others (i.e., children in foster care or in the care of a relative). I said, "No" because these kiddos were not in a homeless or domestic violence shelter. This was hard for me, as someone who loves their birthday. It hurt me to say "no, I can't help to celebrate a kiddo's birthday." However, I did it because I knew if I didn't, we would lose focus and potentially not have the resources to serve the kiddos in our mission. Admittedly, sometimes I would provide a cake out of my personal finances. Remember, I love birthdays.

I often wonder what happens to the moms and kiddos IYBI serves. One day, while at an event, a mom, "Kiesha," recognized me as "The Birthday Lady" who assisted her son three years prior. She and her four kiddos were in one of the domestic shelters that we provided a birthday party for. "Kiesha" joyfully shared the excitement her family felt when we provided her son a fun birthday party. She recalled how her kiddos continued to play with the creative balloons from the balloon artist and the toys all of the kiddos received, as well as the beauty products we gave to her and the other moms. She continued to thank me for the great time It's Your Birthday, Inc. gave her kiddos during a very challenging time for them.

Celebrating birthdays is definitely the fun part. For the first two years, I cried each time a mom would hug me with gratitude because we were able to help her provide her child with a better birthday memory than she could during this unfortunate time for the family. While these moments give me joy to recall, I also remember the tears I cried when I felt I was failing.

Many nights, I would fall asleep thinking, "Why am I putting myself through this? I know nothing about the nonprofit world. I have been in for-profit corporate America all of my career, and my degree is in fashion merchandise!" Then I tell myself, "You aren't doing your degree work, either, so why not continue with this?"

My second big ah-ha moment occurred during 2020—the pandemic. Up until then, I had been "superwoman." I wore many capes at It's Your Birthday, Inc. I was the fundraiser, marketer, volunteer manager, executive director, and administrator. Then, it hit me that I was the single point of failure in the organization.

We were in a pandemic. Kiddos continued to have birthdays. I did whatever I could to ensure they were still celebrated (including masking up and dropping off birthday boxes filled with toys to the shelters' doorsteps). I thought, "What would happen if I became ill?" No more birthday boxes. I knew I had to do something. I didn't want my legacy to be: *Those kiddos were celebrated until the founder could no longer help.* That was not the legacy I wanted, nor an example of a good leader. After all, I teach leaders how to be good leaders, and here I was not modeling the behavior.

My first task was to list all of the things I do. Then, note which things I needed to continue doing in my role and what tasks to delegate. I was denied several grants, failed at fundraising, and volunteer turnover was high. I wanted to spend more time relationship-building in the community. This is where I shine best. Hiring a part-time admin was first, followed by a grant writer, and getting help with fundraising and marketing. Again, getting people with expertise in those areas was key.

Since this change (and we are still developing), I sleep better at night knowing I don't need to be superwoman because there is a team that believes in our mission and has the same vision for growth as me. Each person wears their own cape.

Many people ask me what's next.

My vision is for It's Your Birthday, Inc. to provide a fun and memorable birthday experience for children in homeless and domestic violence shelters **across the United States of America**.

Our first task is to ensure IYBI has the right infrastructure in place—people, funding, and technology. As an entrepreneur, I have always liked the mantra "Go slow to go fast." It's been eleven years, and we have been very strategic with our growth. It's now time to pick up the pace.

We are on our way to achieving this vision with our new shelter partner in West Chester, Pennsylvania, in 2025.

As the founder and Chief Birthday Officer of It's Your Birthday, Inc. (IYBI), Rolanda Finch is responsible for strategic planning and day-to-day operations.

Loving her birthday, in 2014, she wanted children in shelters to have a better memory on their birthday. To make a difference, Rolanda founded It's Your Birthday, Inc. The mission is to create a fun and memorable birthday experience for children in homeless and domestic violence shelters. The services provided by IYBI provide a sense of normalcy and help children to feel acknowledged and special on their birthday.

Operating with mostly volunteers, since 2014, Rolanda has successfully provided more than 2,800 children with a better birthday memory in 29 shelters in Missouri, Illinois, Indiana, and Pennsylvania.

When she is not working to create normalcy for children in shelters, she is a director of learning and leadership at Rocky Mountain Institute (RMI), where she leads the strategy to enhance skills, drive performance, and align learning initiatives with RMI goals for the 700+ employees.

In her "spare" time, Rolanda enjoys spending time with her husband and extended family, traveling, and attending local festivals.

Please scan the QR code to connect with this author.

G.R.I.T.

Jeff Fitter

A Journey of Passion and Perseverance

The Beginning

I knew at a young age what I wanted in life. I had two passions before I was eighteen—cooking and technology. Here's how I got them: my grandmother, Laverne "Vicky," is one of the most important people in my life. With her, I discovered my first passion; she taught me to cook. She was a demonstrator for Farberware when they introduced their new free-standing convection oven. I would go to her house after school and help prep food, and on the weekends, we'd cook and pass out samples. I think I was all of ten, maybe. I found my second passion in the mid-1980s. Like most teenagers, I thought I had the world by the tail! Growing up, I was always fascinated by computers, and my uncle Dan worked with them and taught a class at a local junior college. I would visit his house often and use his system. This was way before the floppy drive or CDs.

The journey, however, was far from easy. I dropped out of high school twice and never completed college! I learned the hard way that getting into the Information Technology (IT) industry required much more than just hard work and determination, or as most call it, grit! I knew if I wanted to run my own company one day, I had a lot to learn, and the best way was to find a company that would invest in me! My plan was simple: learn a niche IT business, then open restaurants to help people create memories with our offerings and hospitality! Oh boy, did I find that company—and with them, I became the person I am today, gaining all the experience needed to take on the title of business owner.

I spent nearly twenty-five years in various positions within the technology world, retiring in 2017 as the Vice President of Strategy and Product for a technology company that provided services to inmates in prisons and jails. Yep, I fulfilled what many people thought would be my future as a teenager! I went to prison—but they let me out each night, because I was working there!

If at First You Don't Succeed, Try, Try Again!

My first venture was a partnership with my wife, Michelle. We worked to create a company that submitted medical claims to insurance companies. She worked in this industry; I just had to help sell and ensure we had the technical capabilities to get the job done. I think this lasted six, maybe eight months, until both we and our clients realized that most doctors' offices could hire internal staff to process the claims at a much lower cost. The lesson learned: even if you're an expert, that alone doesn't guarantee you'll be paid handsomely for it.

My next venture was providing IT services, things like computer and network hardware setup and support. This was, after all, what I did as my full-time job. Right out of the gate, I was able to leverage my network and land several clients. I had even hired my cousin to help. We eventually had to move on when the travel demands of my full-time job became too intense to allow me to run my business alongside it. Wow, did I learn so much from this experience—one lesson being that your network is very important!

In 2001, I discovered my love for barbeque and fell head-over-heels in love with it! I was on the fast track to something great when I was accepted to a BBQ team that allowed me to walk the stage in Memphis, cooking with them there for the first time. Just a few months later, my neighbors and I started our own team and my first catering company. I had an opportunity to partner with a friend to open a restaurant featuring award-winning BBQ in 2008, and we did it. This turned out to be the best learning experience for me, as it helped me to understand how to juggle my full-time job while also living the dream as a restaurant owner. I bought that business in 2017, and that is where this all became a reality! All in all, I learned that I had a lot to learn before I took the big leap!

The Challenges

Challenges, as defined by me, are life's learning lessons! Challenges are life's way of helping you learn by forcing you to face the consequences that follow your decisions. Sometimes, they're positive and help you along the way. Many times, they're learning lessons—failures—that you must overcome to achieve your goals! For example, my dropping out of school became an obstacle I would have to deal with later in life. As it turns out, completing high school and college is much more than just a diploma; it's your first opportunity to show others your work ethic and ability to persevere.

One of the biggest challenges to date, however, has been the global pandemic. Our restaurant, like all others, was forced to shut down all dine-in service, which is what we're built to do. We had to pivot (insert your best memory of Ross from the *Friends* episode, moving the couch upstairs, yelling "Pivot!"), and man, did we have to do it quickly. Talk about the great unknown. Prices for everything were soaring, and product was not readily available. Everything we knew about the world had changed. And it had changed *FOREVER*!

I wasn't sure I was prepared for what was ahead of me—each day another change and another plan, but I found that I was much more prepared for the challenges than I thought. I had accomplished so much in my corporate life and had learned how to navigate rough waters. One of the first things I learned as an entrepreneur was to surround myself with people who lift me up. Make no mistake about it, I am a smart person, but nowhere near as smart as a room full of my peers and staff! I leveraged that to the best of my ability. I worked daily with my food partner, who educated me about the changes in product availability and pricing. This allowed me to make informed decisions about what we would offer and how to maximize the product we were able to get.

Milestones Achieved

As the months passed, we achieved several milestones that validated our efforts. In 2018, one year into owning the first restaurant, Super Smokers BBQ, we had made substantial changes that led to an 18 percent increase in sales. In 2019, we focused on catering and expanded our offerings to include a food trailer that went to festivals, private events, and the first food truck park to open in the St. Louis area, *9 Mile Garden*. This grew our revenue by another 15 percent over the previous year.

2020 was our most challenging year with the global pandemic, yet it turned out to be our highest revenue year. We were able to leverage our network to become one of about ten restaurants selected to feed first responders daily for several months. At the same time, we offered meals at a discounted price as a way for the public to support the hospital staff who take amazing care of us all every day! The trickle effect of this was amazing. We were able to place large orders from our supplier and work with them to provide product that kept their staff employed. We finished 2020 with double the revenue compared to 2016.

Given our successes to date, we started building our team to help manage and grow the business. Our daughter, Ciarra (CJ), who has been cooking with me since 2006 or so, had graduated from college and decided to work with me full-time. I was incredibly excited, because I had spent so much of her life away due to all my travel. She has a passion for the business and for cooking BBQ that is only matched by her drive to learn it all. She started on pit; she'd been cooking most of the caterings from our small catering company, so she was already well trained. She then quickly transitioned from pit master to shift lead to the restaurant manager. In fact, she's done it all and mastered it. She now manages our financials and back-end process and helps the team operate two restaurants and three food trucks! She's become an amazing woman, mother, wife, and a critical part of our team that I hope one day takes on the legacy to take it places I never could!

We are a family business, with my wife Michelle, daughters Brittni and CJ, along with their spouses, all working to make our business thrive. Michelle has a full-time job and still finds time to help me with the daily challenges, while also working closely with CJ on the financials. Brittni handles most of our catering while also working a full-time job. Our grandkids—Elliot (5), Taytum (2), and Walker (1)—are even involved. Elliot is an amazing host, Taytum carries the menus for him, and Walker just smiles and melts hearts.

We expanded our staff to include our first chef, who happened to be a BBQ guy and an even better person. With Chef Jamie's help, we expanded our offerings to include Cajun cuisine and opened a second location in 2021: Super Smokers BBQ + Cajun! Sadly, due to the changing world, this location only lasted about two and a half years. But Jaime has stuck with us, and today he runs all back-of-house operations at both restaurants.

Each milestone was a testament to our hard work, strategic planning, and unwavering belief in our vision. In 2022, we purchased another legacy restaurant, one close to our home and even closer to our hearts. *Case and Bucks* was founded in 1992, and Michelle and I started eating there in 1993. Our family used it for every gathering at my grandma's house, and

I fell in love with the wings there. When the opportunity to take it over came, it was only a matter of time—and money—before it became ours.

It's now 2025, and we've had to pivot yet again. Costs have risen so sharply that we're struggling to sustain them long-term. So, we opened a restaurant within a restaurant and branded it *Papa's Diner*. Yep, you guessed it—we're serving breakfast all day, along with some amazing scratch-made dishes, including our award-winning BBQ. You see, if you want to be successful, you have to be willing to listen, learn, grow—and most importantly, be willing to apply what you've learned.

I don't want to mislead you. All this happened with so many setbacks that I could write a book on just those, but this section is "Milestones Achieved." It's important to remember that you must celebrate the daily wins and have a short-term memory with the setbacks. Learn from them and move on. Nobody is going to give you a damn thing, and most importantly, you must always dig deep and stay true to who you are if you're to persevere through all the ups and downs you'll face.

The Future

Looking back, my journey has been a rollercoaster of emotions, filled with highs and lows, successes and failures. But through it all, my passion for hospitality and my desire to make a difference have remained constant. My journey is far from over. The entrepreneurial landscape is constantly evolving, and staying relevant requires continuous learning and adaptation. My goal is to keep pushing the boundaries, exploring new possibilities, and inspiring the next generation of entrepreneurs to chase their dreams with unwavering determination. My journey is a testament to the power of perseverance and the impact of a strong support system. Without my wife and kids, I would not have made it this far. As I continue this path, I'm reminded that the essence of entrepreneurship lies not just in the destination but in the journey itself.

Jeff spent nearly twenty-five years in the technology sector, culminating in his role as Vice President of Strategy and Product for a company providing services to prison inmates. However, his true calling lay in the culinary world. In 2001, Jeff discovered his love for barbecue, leading him to start a catering company and eventually open his own restaurant.

Throughout his journey, Jeff faced numerous challenges, including the impact of a global pandemic. However, his resilience and ability to adapt allowed him to overcome these obstacles and achieve significant milestones. Under his leadership, Super Smokers BBQ saw substantial growth, and Jeff expanded his business to include multiple restaurants and food trucks.

Jeff's success is a family affair, with his wife Michelle, daughters Ciarra (CJ) and Brittni, and their spouses all playing integral roles in the business. Together, they have built a thriving enterprise that continues to evolve and grow.

Please scan the QR code to connect with this author.

G.R.I.T.®

Tim Hebel

The Entrepreneurial Journey Takes Grit—and Lots of It

The entrepreneurial journey takes grit—and lots of it. Many people daydream about becoming a business owner. They envision the success and the potential perks: setting your own hours, being your own boss, making the rules. What those daydreams usually leave out are the trials and tribulations that inevitably appear at every stage of growing a business. The reality check that comes with business ownership quickly extinguishes any "grass is greener" mentality.

Only those who embrace G.R.I.T. (growth, resilience, intention, and tenacity) can fully harness the lessons that come from mistakes, bad luck, and hard-earned wisdom. When you lean into those experiences, they shape you into someone greater than you were before.

My own journey has been full of challenges, and each one has made me a better person. There are three lessons that stand out in particular because each one fundamentally changed me. In the first, my hubris was replaced by humility. In the second, physical symptoms of stress became a wake-up call—and a turning point for my long-term health. And in the third, which is still unfolding today, I›m learning how to stay tenacious during tough times that are beyond my control. Embracing grit has made me a better leader, a better father, and a better man.

From Hubris to Humility

My desire to be an entrepreneur started early. By late high school, I'd already made a major decision: even though I wanted to start a business, I wasn't going to waste time going to business school. I was too smart for that. Yeah, hubris was my name, and humility was not my game.

Academic success has come easily to me for most of my life. Awards and accolades piled up, each one another brick in my own, personal Tower of Babel. I decided to pursue a degree in Ocean Engineering, mainly because so few students graduated in that field each year. My thinking was: the less competition, the easier it would be to carve out a niche and build a successful business.

But moving from the Midwest to South Florida at eighteen came with plenty of distractions. My straight-A track record quickly crumbled. Eventually, I moved back to St. Louis, switched my major to Computer Science, and tried to recover from my first major failed plan. Strike one against the ego.

During my time at the University of Missouri–St. Louis, I started building websites for family and friends while continuing my coursework. Word spread. Referrals started coming in, and before long, I had more work than I could handle on my own. So, I hired a few of my classmates— my first employees—and we started building something.

Fast forward thirteen years: that side hustle is still my primary business and career. I didn't plan it this way, but as we all know, life has a funny way of rewriting your plans. Beanstalk Web Solutions was born out of opportunity, not strategy. And yet, it took off.

Soon, my ego started to make a comeback. Here I was, twenty-three years old, running a business with an office, employees, and a decent income—and I hadn't even finished my degree yet. I remember thinking, *"See? I didn't need that business degree after all. I'm smart. I'll figure it out."*

And that's when humility made its long-overdue entrance. The truth hit me hard: there were a lot of things I didn't know. Managing people was difficult, and it definitely didn't come naturally. I hated hard conversations and avoided them, often to my own detriment. I thought I knew how to read a P&L statement. I believed I understood balance sheets. But in reality, I was flying blind in many areas. Some fundamental business classes definitely would've helped. Instead of letting these realizations knock me down, I leaned into them. I embraced grit.

I joined the Small Business Association's Emerging Leaders program, a course that teaches business fundamentals to small business owners. At first, I figured I wouldn't learn much. Classic me. But the program ended up being incredibly eye-opening. I also began working on my leadership skills, especially in areas like people management. That process took years, but eventually I embraced the idea of elevating and delegating. Today, I have a team of leaders who are far better at managing people than I am, and that's one of my proudest achievements.

When Stress Becomes Physical

The next trial hit me a few years into running the business, and in some ways, I'm still navigating it today. By that time, the company was growing fast, and I was still working on finishing my degree. I was down to just a few challenging capstone courses, but they were intense—high-level programming and math. Meanwhile, Beanstalk was demanding more than a full-time commitment. Mentally, I thought I was doing okay, but I noticed something disturbing: my stress was manifesting in a very physical way.

We now understand that stress is a major contributor to serious health issues like heart disease, cancer, and more. Doctors spend a lot of time urging patients to reduce stress in sustainable, healthy ways. But I wasn't listening. I didn't realize just how much damage I was doing.

It all came to a head when I started experiencing symptoms that pointed to diabetes. I scheduled a doctor's visit, and my initial blood sugar levels were deep in the danger zone. After further testing, the doctors concluded that I didn't actually have diabetes, but my body was mimicking it. As it turns out, extreme stress can cause cortisol levels in the body to spike and block the effectiveness of insulin. Basically, I was so stressed that my body was acting like it was diabetic.

That was my wake-up call. At the time, I didn't yet have a family. Today, I'm lucky to have a wife and three beautiful daughters. But even back then, I knew I wanted a family, and I wanted to be around for them. No business, no level of success, is worth a heart attack or stroke in your forties.

So once again, I turned to grit. I began making small, incremental changes, most of them seemingly insignificant at first. But over time, those changes added up. Some of the habits I adopted include:

- Turning off mobile notifications

- Leaving my phone on silent

- Consistent exercise

- Meditation, sauna, and stretching

- Healthier food choices

- Driving slower

- Not reading emails on vacation

- Not taking things so personally

Each one alone didn't fix everything, but together, they transformed the way I handle stress. I'm still not perfect. But I'm miles from where I was.

If you're reading this and haven't had your own wake-up call yet, don't wait for one. Someone in a networking group I was part of used to say, *"What good is your wealth without your health?"* That one stuck with me.

Tenacity in the Face of Uncertainty

The last trial I'll share is one that's still in progress. For the first eight or nine years, my business was on a steady upward trajectory. Every year was better than the last. Leads were flowing, our sales process was smooth, and even the pandemic didn't slow us down. In fact, it accelerated our growth.

Then, about two and a half years ago, everything changed. What many now call the "Agency Recession" hit, and it hit hard. Marketing agencies across the board began experiencing the same problems: leads dried up and sales pipelines froze. Prospects weren't saying yes or no—they were just stuck. Out of fifteen agency owners I regularly talk to, all but one saw declining revenue that year.

Why? It seems to come down to a mix of economic uncertainty and changing market behavior. The rise of Artificial Intelligence didn't help, but the bigger issue was a general decline in business confidence. Marketing budgets are often the first to get cut when people fear a downturn, whether or not one actually materializes.

There were times over the past couple of years when I felt truly discouraged. My president and I have had the same conversation over and over again: *"Are we doing something wrong?"* But each time, we remind ourselves, we're not alone. Our peers are in the same boat.

And so, I keep coming back to grit. This is where tenacity really comes into play. I don't know when the tide will turn, but I do know it will. If we stay resilient and intentional with our decisions, the growth will come back.

Closing Thoughts

The trials and tribulations of entrepreneurship are no joke. But they're also some of the most rewarding experiences a person can go through—if you're willing to learn from them. Grit has shaped me in ways I never expected. Each mistake and misstep has become a stepping stone. I've learned more from my failures than I ever learned from my wins. And that knowledge—the self-awareness, the growth, the humility—drives me every day. I know that if I keep going, stay focused, and remain tenacious, I'll continue becoming a wiser man. And with that wisdom, I'll be able to give more to my business, my family, and the people I serve.

Tim Hebel is the founder and CEO of Beanstalk Web Solutions, a full-service digital marketing and web design agency in St. Louis that he built from a college side-hustle into a thriving business. A graduate of the University of Missouri–St. Louis, Tim was honored as the commencement speaker for UMSL's 2016 spring graduation. His entrepreneurial journey has earned him recognition as a *Titan 100 — St. Louis 2024* honoree and a place on the *St. Louis Business Journal's 40 Under 40* list in 2021. Tim has also been named among the "Top 100 St. Louisans You Should Know to Succeed in Business" and received the "Future 50 Award" as one of the top small companies in St. Louis. Beyond his professional achievements, Tim is a dedicated father to three daughters, bringing the same passion and commitment to family life that have guided his business success.

Please scan the QR code to connect with this author.

G.R.I.T.

Katie Jimenez

Turning Childhood Obstacles into Entrepreneurial Successes

I lived in Washington Park, Illinois, until I was around eight or nine years old before moving to Missouri. My father is from Tibana, Colombia, and he immigrated to the United States in his twenties. He became a citizen when I was a young girl, even though he only had a third-grade education. In the seventies and eighties, and even today, it was difficult for a brown-skinned man who spoke broken English to find acceptance. My mother came from Washington Park in East St. Louis, Illinois, and often shared stories about segregation and bomb threats in our community. She graduated from St. Theresa's all-girls school and later attended business school, where she excelled as an accountant, showcasing her remarkable aptitude for numbers. Being a woman in a man's world, she had fewer options than women do today. I witnessed her strength and perseverance firsthand, and I believe I naturally inherited my spirited personality from both my parents, who worked hard their entire lives.

I faced challenges in school due to learning disabilities and extreme ADHD. Having ADHD and likely some dyslexia made it incredibly difficult for me to focus and read. Eventually, I dropped out at 16, enjoying a vibrant life until I unexpectedly became pregnant. Supporting my family became essential, which led me to pursue a career in construction, where pay and health insurance were appealing.

From 1998 to 2000, I attended Ranken Technical College while relying on welfare and working part-time at a bar to make ends meet. I graduated on a Thursday and had a job by Monday, with the pay and insurance I was seeking. I began my career in the union in August 2000, proudly ranking among the top ten women to join the union. I vividly remember being the only woman on job sites for years, facing looks, stares, and jokes. You have to be a certain type of person to work in construction, and being a minority woman only added to the thickness of my skin. No matter what happened, I didn't stop. Most of the guys were great—I'd grown up with many of them—and I had some of the best times. The good always outweighed the bad.

Over the years, I took classes after work at the hall whenever I could and completed my advanced apprenticeship. After September 11, 2000, I returned to Ranken and earned a two-year certification in HVAC. I launched Avid Electric and Communication in 2016, driven by the necessity of having a registered company to obtain my license for the required testing. To help finance this venture, my dad generously loaned me just under $7,000, which served as the initial capital I needed to kickstart the business.

After laying the groundwork, I successfully secured my first contract in 2017, worth $20,000, focused on fire alarm installations. Making the leap from being an employee to becoming a business owner was a transformative experience for me.

In my company's inaugural year, Avid generated an impressive $300,000 in revenue. Over the next three years, my earnings consistently ranged between $270,000 and just shy of $800,000 annually, reflecting the growth and success of my business as it established itself within the industry.

Things changed for me in my third year of business when I met Julie Ledbetter for the first time at a coffee shop. I had never heard of her and had no idea who she was. She told me she wanted to mentor me and explained that she owned a construction company and understood the challenges I was facing. I accepted her offer, and that's when I began to grasp the financial side of my business.

I had been keeping track of entries, but I wasn't trained and certainly wasn't an accountant. Julie spent countless hours with me—days and weeks—going over accounting work-in-progress sheets, true costs, true profits, P&L statements, and balance sheets. This continued for years. Julie became my mentor and my friend; she understood the ups and downs, the struggles, and the pain.

She would take my rough calls on days when I didn't want to leave the house or even get out of bed. She listened without judgment and helped me find the strength to push through the toughest times in both my life and career. Julie is incredibly important to me; she saw potential in me that I couldn't see in myself, and often knew what my next move should be before I did. No one has ever helped me in the way Julie did. She had nothing to gain from it; her support came straight from the heart. All she wanted was to see me succeed, and for that, I am forever grateful.

Julie and I quickly realized that Avid required mentoring from an experienced electrical contractor to elevate my business. Julie introduced me to several contractors, including Guarantee Electrical Company. Guarantee is the oldest and largest electrical contracting company in the St. Louis, Missouri area. The leadership of Guarantee, including Dave Gralike, president, believes in genuine mentoring; their goal is to ensure their diverse partners become stronger companies. Here was the president of the largest electrical company making time for me, and the name Gralike is one of the most well-respected names in construction.

Guarantee assisted me in many ways; their low-voltage senior estimator, Tim Huston, authenticated my labor units and pricing. Nick Arb, vice president of Strategy, guided me through the 8A process and invited me to attend outreach and business development events.

I worked with many Guarantee project managers, specifically Rob Truebe and Matt Schmid. The project managers did not treat me like a subcontractor; they considered me a teammate. We held monthly meetings to review contracts and various financial matters. I gained valuable insights into financials, bidding, customer relations, and efficient performance. I don't know of any other company in this field that offers as much mentorship. Guarantee always kept their word throughout the process, they recognized my potential, and they fulfilled their goal: Avid is a stronger company due to Guarantee's mentorship.

As I was gearing up for the largest contracts of my career, I went through the loss of my mom. It was a year of watching her decline and not knowing how to stop the pain. That experience forced me to confront a lot of demons from my past. When she passed, I only took two hours off. I had multiple large contracts over a million dollars and was preparing for the largest contract of my career: a $1.3 million deal.

That was the toughest challenge of my life. Managing such significant work while dealing with the loss of my mother was incredibly hard. I questioned everything in my life; it crushed me and broke my heart. I found myself working relentlessly, working in the field with my tools only to sneak away to an empty room for a brief breakdown before returning to the chaos of phone calls, customer questions, and meetings I needed to be prepared for.

I had no time to grieve my mom's loss, and that was truly difficult. But I persevered and made it through the biggest contract of my career. I juggled numerous responsibilities: payroll, certified payroll, accounts payable and receivable, estimating, service calls, change orders, project management, and schedules. I would go into meetings looking professional from the waist up while wearing jeans and boots underneath. After the meeting was over, I would turn around and head back to the job site.

I often found myself working on ladders with my phone tucked into my shirt pocket, taking calls. I would even fall asleep with my laptop on my lap, working seven days a week. Even when I took a vacation, I was still tied to my laptop and phone, handling meetings and calls.

Working with my hands and knowing numbers became my superpower. I didn't realize it when I was young, but my ADHD transformed into a strength, particularly in the business world. I may not have had much formal education, but I had an unyielding drive and never allowed obstacles to stop me.

Statistically, I wasn't supposed to make it. Here I was, a little girl from East St. Louis, Illinois, with parents from different worlds. I was a single mom, and yet the most successful electrical company wanted Avid on their projects. Avid has worked on some of the biggest, most challenging, and highest-profile contracts in the St. Louis, Missouri area.

I'm the first Hispanic woman electrical contractor in low voltage, from what I know, in the Midwest. I am one of the top ten women to come into the union. I'm the owner of a company that generates between $2 million and $4 million a year in revenue. I employ people. I provide health benefits. I am a minority-owned contractor who runs a solid union construction company.

Katie Jimenez is the owner of Avid Electric and Communication, a woman-and-minority-owned, family-operated, low-voltage electrical contracting firm based in St. Louis, Missouri. Founded in 2016, her company specializes in fire alarm systems, access control, data network cabling, security camera installations, and other telecommunications services for commercial clients throughout Missouri.

Katie is a graduate of Ranken Technical College with a degree in Industrial Electricity and Electronics (2000) and also holds an HVAC degree. And is NICET 3 in Fire Alarm Systems. She has been in the electrical field since 1998 and works as a union contractor.

As a first-generation Latina, Katie is passionate about breaking barriers and growing a "woman-dominated shop." She is deeply committed to staying current on fire, building, and electrical codes to ensure safety and compliance.

Katie balances her professional ambitions with life as a single mom and is proud of her heritage and the consultative, high-quality service her company provides to clients. She has earned Avid Electric DBE/MBE/WBE certifications, reflecting her dedication to diversity and excellence in the electrical contracting industry.

Please scan the QR code to connect with this author.

G.R.I.T.

Chip Smith

Keep Things in Perspective

I've aspired to be an entrepreneur for as long as I can remember, and my path to successful entrepreneurship took decades and a multitude of failed ideas and attempts. While I use the term "successful" very loosely, I am very fortunate to have helped start five businesses that all exist today, four of which we successfully exited. Being an entrepreneur is incredibly fun, stressful, and rewarding, and grit is essential for success, regardless of how you choose to define it.

This journey we are on is about perspective: There are nearly eight billion people on Earth—one of approximately 200 billion planets in the Milky Way and an estimated twenty-one sextillion planets in the universe. Reflecting on my journey, I have concluded that my professional successes and failures are insignificant in the grand scheme of life. Success or failure, unequivocally, my greatest blessing is being able to be myself and having family and friends who love and don't judge. If you're dealing with professional adversity, try to zoom out, focus on what you're grateful for, and keep things in perspective. I often lean into a quote shared by a great friend and mentor who immigrated alone from Greece in the 1970s: "Life is short and unpredictable." Please remember everyone is on their own short journey. Be kind. Enjoy it. And try to help others enjoy it too. We never know what tomorrow may bring.

My upbringing is incredibly important to both my entrepreneurial aspirations and my path to getting here. My childhood was filled with large, frequent gatherings and road trips, and members of my family—particularly my grandfathers, dad, and uncles—never met a stranger. Whether it was a server in a restaurant, a gas station attendant, or another patron, the habit of striking up a conversation with genuine interest, kindness, and a touch of humor vividly sticks with me to this day, and is a character trait I have long tried to emulate.

I am fortunate to have grown up with such a close and supportive extended family, and their influence has been unparalleled in helping me navigate life. The defining themes of those gatherings—and countless interactions with strangers—were simple yet powerful: family, fun, empathy, kindness, generosity, authenticity, and humor. These values have shaped my outlook on life, and they have played an incredibly significant role in my relationships, which are the source of all good things in my life. Relationships are the source of my wife (and thus my daughter), and the many friends, bosses, partners, team members, and advisors who have been part of my journey—for all of whom I am beyond grateful.

I've been exposed to—and inspired by—many entrepreneurs, and it's also in my family's DNA. While he may not have been considered very successful by traditional monetary standards, my paternal grandfather was a consummate entrepreneur. As a teen not yet old enough to drive, he bought a jon boat and sold popcorn boat rides on the Meramec River. He later started a Sinclair gas station and bought his parents' confectionery store in Pacific, Missouri, which fed my dad's own entrepreneurial spirit. After twenty years in banking, my dad transitioned into buyouts and private investments, building an incredibly diverse portfolio—from elevator inspections and chain manufacturing to stuffing your own bears. He also helped my uncle purchase a manufacturing company, providing additional fuel for my own entrepreneurial aspirations. My enterprising neighbor—now the CEO of a multi-billion-dollar financial services firm—had us selling lemonade, comic books, and baseball cards before I could even read. His father was also an entrepreneur, including the creation of Bingo Brain. Other inspiring entrepreneurs include former bosses, clients, friends, landlords, past and current business partners, and my forum mates from the Entrepreneur's Organization. One of my friends, mentors, and business partners is the co-founder of Charter/Spectrum, who passed along some great wisdom: "Choose your business partner(s) as carefully as you choose your spouse." If you know my wife, that set an unreachable bar for my business partners!

One common theme among the entrepreneurs who have inspired me is a willingness to take risks and to fail. My grandfather experienced plenty of adversity. While I didn't witness it personally, I've heard the stories and benefited from his resilience and tenacity. Some of those setbacks were tied to a struggle with alcohol, which he fortunately overcame. Unfortunately, that struggle also seems to be in my DNA; it has led to my own challenges, and at times, continues to be a struggle. Thankfully, I have unconditional love and support as I try to conquer this challenge as well. My dad and his partners also had to shut down businesses. I vividly remember how painful and gut-wrenching that experience was for him.

My friend from Greece moved to the United States around age eighteen, enrolled at SLU, only to drop out after realizing the $200 tuition was for a semester, not the entire year. After bussing tables at the University Club, he bought a truck, built a successful logistics business, and then found himself in bankruptcy.

Another, much more important, theme is that these inspiring entrepreneurs kept going in the face of adversity. My friend from Greece rebuilt his business, and it thrives today. Through each pivotal experience—whether success or failure—they learned, grew, and persisted. They have been incredible examples of the importance of growth and resilience.

Above all else, these influences in my life demonstrated what's most important: family, being kind, and trying to enjoy this journey together.

With the intention of someday becoming my own boss, I had an aversion to reading schoolbooks and sitting in class. I loved engaging with people, immersing myself in new experiences, and trying to drum up the next business idea—or finding a business to buy. Some of my early pitches during school included a tortilla manufacturing business, a roll-up of RainSoft water dealerships, and a Buffalo Wild Wings franchise. Despite considerable research, effort, and what I considered compelling proposals, all my efforts failed. I never successfully launched or acquired a business while in school, but I did manage to graduate from Denison University—with mediocre grades, a Bachelor of Arts in economics, great friends, and a tremendous number of experiences and memories (though many are a little fuzzy!).

In true econ-major fashion, I landed my first full-time job at NASA in Washington, D.C. It was an incredible position—challenging, fast-paced, and filled with exposure to a remarkable leader, as well as pioneers and innovators who inspired not just NASA but a global contingency of space enthusiasts, scientists, and humans in general. I've always had a passion for—and fascination with—the cosmos, and working with NASA further cemented my belief that we should think bigger. We are just one of many important species on a shared planet with a finite lifespan. When viewed at that scale, I really don't have problems.

I loved my time at NASA, but I wanted to return home and become my own boss or get into private equity, a near-impossible task with no money and mediocre grades. With no intention of making a career practicing law, I enrolled at Saint Louis University (SLU) for a four-year JD/MBA program in the fall of 2002.

In my first year, I landed a paid internship at a great boutique law firm, and soon thereafter, I joined the University Club, initially for its gym and squash courts but mostly for the opportunity to network. I quickly decided I was better off working—getting paid to gain real-world experience—or working out and socializing at the University Club, than sitting in class or reading books. With a deep desire to "be my own boss," I was constantly brainstorming business ideas, chasing businesses, or networking with and learning from business owners and executives. I befriended the man who is now my father-in-law, himself a lifelong entrepreneur. At a holiday party, he introduced me to his oldest daughter, who was also attending SLU Law. Thanks to my tendency to miss class, I stretched a four-year program into something longer and ended up graduating the same year as my wife.

My wife and I married in 2007. Fast forward five years: she was an assistant prosecuting attorney, and I was a part-time lawyer, real estate broker, insurance agent, and, mostly, still an aspiring entrepreneur. With no kids, an incredibly understanding and supportive wife, a little bit of money, and a lot more of pent-up desire and intention, I decided it was time to take the leap and founded Greenleaf Capital Partners with my younger brother. Named after the street we grew up on—with our enterprising neighbor—Greenleaf began by advising businesses on capital formation, acquisitions, and divestitures. We evolved into an investment and management firm that backs a variety of businesses, including startups, led by proven and passionate management teams. Our first investment—in a startup insurance brokerage with amazing co-founders and a stellar team—was incredible!

Not long after launching Greenleaf, I experienced one of the highlights of my life: starting ATIS with my dad and brother. Founded on values that were instilled throughout childhood, we hired our first employee on December 10, 2012, and began performing elevator safety inspections in January 2013. We had a vision and a purpose, and we surrounded ourselves with smart people who were committed to authenticity, empathy, and taking care of our team, so they, in turn, would take care of our customers.

Despite exhaustive planning, ATIS didn't go anything like we had envisioned. Within the first month, we found ourselves in litigation with a $4+ billion conglomerate and sustained financial losses that exceeded twice our projections. One of many lessons learned: Take your best guess at the cost of starting a business—and double it!

Along with sleepless nights worrying about making payroll, I remember February 10, 2014, as if it were yesterday. With litigation behind us, the day began with excitement: our new president was starting that day. Shortly after arriving at the office, I took a call from my mom and learned, through cries and screams, that my cousin—very much like a brother—had been found dead by his parents in their R&D facility. His death was a tragedy unlike anything I had experienced, nor anything that I can, or want to, imagine for my aunt and uncle. They and their daughters have demonstrated unimaginable resilience and have permanently altered my perspective on adversity, strength, and what's important in life.

At ATIS, we stayed committed to our values and continued to build an amazing team I had the honor of leading for over a decade. ATIS pioneered vertical transportation management, and thanks to the team's focus on being the employer and provider of choice, we became the largest provider of elevator inspections, consulting, and managed services in North America. We closed a second majority recap in late 2024, and with our new partner and new leadership, the future looks unbelievably bright for ATIS.

ATIS was a remarkable journey—indescribably fun, stressful, and rewarding. However, it was in the midst of that journey—"alone at the top," with shaky confidence, and considerable stress—when my life changed forever, further cementing my outlook on life. Born in May

2017, our daughter is the greatest gift, joy, and a daily reminder of what truly matters in this crazy world—and how good life can be!

Reflecting on my journey, I am indescribably grateful for the relationships that have enriched my life and the opportunities that have allowed me to grow. I encourage you to reflect on your own journey and try to keep both your successes and your challenges in perspective! Oh…. lastly, please be the nice kid. In business and in life, kindness is often the trait people remember most. It costs nothing, means everything, and opens more doors than talent ever will.

Chip Smith was born and raised in St. Louis, Missouri, and is the middle of five children. After earning a B.A. in economics from Denison University, he began his career at NASA, where he worked in the Office of the Administrator, the Office of the CFO, and Public Affairs. He later enrolled at Saint Louis University, completing a JD/MBA degree. After practicing law for five years, Chip co-founded Greenleaf Capital Partners with his brother, investing in businesses, including startups, led by proven management teams. Chip is married with one daughter, and they enjoy traveling, camping, and riding horses or golf carts.

Please scan the QR code to connect with this author.

G.R.I.T.®

Todd Wallis

Problems Are a Good Thing

"In the middle of difficulty lies opportunity."
—Albert Einstein

Breaking Down and Building Up

As I approached and passed my 50th birthday, I found myself reflecting on the journey that led me here. From a curious kid tinkering in my dad's garage to the founder of a marketing agency, one lesson stands out: problems are a good thing. It might sound counterintuitive, but every challenge I've faced has shaped me, giving me new tools to succeed. Before I knew anything about business, I learned this lesson in the most unexpected place, helping my father fix things around the house.

My Dad's Tools

Some of my earliest memories are of tagging along with Dad on weekend repair jobs. If something broke, especially on one of our vehicles, Dad seldom called a mechanic; he was determined to figure it out himself. I remember one summer afternoon when our tan and brown Ford F-150 was running rough, and Dad decided it needed the timing adjusted. He headed down to the basement and came back holding this wild-looking device I'd never seen before. It was silver and shaped like something out of a sci-fi movie; it was an engine timing light. I watched as he hooked it up to the truck, the strobe flashing like a laser while he made some adjustments. At around ten years old, I was amazed! Dad was an aeronautical engineer by day, but out in the driveway, he was just the guy who somehow knew how to fix everything.

As we worked side-by-side in the garage, the smell of motor oil in the air and KMOX talk radio playing softly in the background, I held the flashlight and tried to keep up. Curious, I asked, "Dad, why do you have so many tools?" He wiped his hands on a rag, grinned, and said, "Because I've had so many things break on me!" At the time, I laughed, but that idea stuck with me. Every time something went wrong—a leaky pipe, a broken fence, a car that wouldn't start—it forced Dad to learn something new and, often, to buy a new tool. By the time I was a teenager, our garage shelves were lined with gadgets and gear for every kind of fix. Each one told a story; something had broken, needed building, or had to be figured out.

The lesson was simple: every problem solved added something to his collection; the right tool for the job. Back then, it was physical equipment. Later in life, I began to recognize the mental and emotional resources I was building with each challenge I faced. My father never sat me down and said, "Problems are good, son." He didn't need to. His example made it clear: every setback carried a hidden benefit, a new skill gained, a new approach discovered, and the growing confidence that we could handle whatever came next. That mindset became the backbone of how I deal with challenges today. I didn't fully understand it as a kid, but those hot afternoons in the garage were shaping me into the kind of entrepreneur who runs *toward* problems instead of *away* from them.

Third Time's the Charm

Fast-forward a few decades: I'm now the president and founder of INBOUND BLEND, a digital marketing agency started in 2017. It's actually the third company I've launched; what can I say, the entrepreneurial bug bit early and hasn't let go. By the time I launched the agency, I had already learned a ton from my previous ventures, most of it the hard way.

My first company, launched in my twenties with my good friend Chris Kubicek, was a product we invented called *Pictails*, a picture frame with a bendable tail designed to attach to bed rails. We came up with it to help patients in hospitals and nursing homes keep photos of loved ones close by. It was meaningful work, and while we didn't scale it the way we had hoped, it taught me so much about product development, solving real problems, and how deeply design can impact people.

In my thirties, I launched a video production business. We were proud of the work we did, everything from product launch videos for Xerox to training videos for the U.S. Marines. But we never quite figured out how to build consistent monthly recurring revenue. That made growth unpredictable and eventually unsustainable. Still, that company gave me hands-on experience in managing teams, storytelling under pressure, and serving high-level clients with complex needs.

By the time INBOUND BLEND came along, I wasn't starting from scratch; I was 42 years old, and I was bringing with me real-world lessons, earned perspective, and what felt like a garage full of tools gathered from every misstep and win along the way. Today, the agency is thriving, and I'm convinced it's because of those accumulated experiences. When something goes sideways on a project, or a campaign doesn't perform the way we expected, my team will tell you they've heard me say it a hundred times: *"Problems are a good thing."* It's practically a motto around here. It always gets a few eye rolls and laughs, but it's real; because every problem we face is just another opportunity in disguise.

This philosophy shapes how we serve our clients too. In the marketing world, clients come to us with pain points: "Our website isn't converting leads," or "We're not reaching the right audience." Essentially, they bring us their problems. And here's a fundamental insight for any entrepreneur: clients pay you to solve their problems. If our clients didn't have any issues or pain, the phone wouldn't ring, and INBOUND BLEND wouldn't exist. Each project is our chance to fix something, to apply our tools, and maybe even acquire new ones. My team has learned to welcome client challenges instead of dreading them. A campaign underperforming? Great! It means we have an opportunity to dig in, get creative, and make it better. A website redesign more complex than anticipated? Fantastic! We'll come out of it with new technical skills or insights. Just as my dad's leaky pipes justified buying a better wrench, a tough client project might push us to learn a new marketing platform or analytics tool. In the end, we not only solve the client's issue but also add that capability to our repertoire.

Sleep On It

I wasn't always good at this. In my early career, I had a bad habit of grinding late into the night on tough problems, thinking more hours would force a solution. More often than not, I just ended up exhausted with nothing to show for it. Now I do the opposite.

One of the best strategies I've learned is knowing when to step away and reset. For me, that often means a good night's sleep. If I'm stuck on a problem or a big decision, I intentionally set it aside overnight. It's amazing how often a solution pops into my head fresh the next morning, as if my brain kept working on the puzzle while I slept. Time and again, I've found that a night of sleep brings clarity that an extra five frantic hours at the desk never would.

Another practice I swear by is scheduling regular moments of what is called "no time." By that, I mean periods with no meetings, no emails, no pressing tasks, just quiet time set aside to do nothing "productive" on the surface. It could be an hour sitting with a cup of coffee, taking a walk, or simply turning off my phone and thinking. In these intentional moments of silence, my mind is free to wander, and that's often when creative ideas or solutions to complex challenges finally surface. In the hustle of running a business, deliberately carving out time to pause can feel illogical, but it's incredibly valuable. My best ideas, and the clearest perspective on tough issues, tend to emerge when I'm not actively "working" on them.

Both the reset and "no time" are about giving yourself permission to pause. Stepping away from a problem, for a night, an hour, or even just a few deep breaths, can be the key to solving it. It's in these quiet gaps that all the experience and tools you've gathered can connect in new ways and reveal the answer.

Embracing Every Problem

Looking back, I'm thankful the road wasn't smooth. The setbacks, the stumbles, the hard lessons; they all pushed me to get better. They didn't just shape my business; they shaped me. And now, I get to pass some of that along. As a father of three, I try to share those lessons with my kids. When they hit a wall, whether it's school, sports, or just life, I remind them that the struggle itself is part of the reward. I'm not always sure it lands in the moment, but I hope it sinks in over time.

For me, that's the real truth behind building a business: problems aren't the detours; they're the path. I've learned that over and over again, whether it was fixing a timing issue on an old Ford with my dad or troubleshooting a marketing campaign that just wouldn't convert. When you hit the next challenge that makes you want to throw something or walk away, pause for a second. Think back to that idea that's carried me this far: problems are a good thing. They're not just headaches; they're invitations. And solving them? That's where the growth happens. That's where your best work comes from.

Todd Wallis is the president and founder of INBOUND BLEND, a digital marketing agency recognized in *St. Louis Small Business Monthly's* Future 50 Companies and named one of the "100 St. Louisans to Know." A U.S. Army veteran, Todd put himself through college, studying marketing at Southern Illinois University Carbondale. Over the years, he's built multiple companies, including a video production firm and a new product startup, each teaching him valuable lessons in resilience and creative problem-solving. Today, he leads INBOUND BLEND with the same grit and curiosity forged in his dad's garage, turning challenges into opportunities and helping businesses grow with intention. He lives in Ballwin, Missouri, with his wife, Katie, daughter Cassidy, and twin sons, Cole and Carter.

Please scan the QR code to connect with this author.

G.R.I.T.

Amanda Wibbenmeyer

Of Course You Did

How did I get here? For the last 20 years, I have been leading teams in retail. Most recently, more than 1,500 people across a few states for a Fortune 40 Company…and then all of a sudden, I'm leading a team of three in a 2,500-square-foot studio.

Party planning and making thoughtful gifts were a passion of mine. I often challenged myself to make videos, themed meetings, custom gifts, epic swag, and over-coordinated birthday parties with any spare moment. Regularly, I would arrive with some type of creation, and friends and family would always say in unison, "Of course you did!"

I exited my fast-paced leadership lifestyle to be more present for my growing boys. I harnessed my hobbies and transitioned them into the ultimate passion project—business ownership!

Through much research, I found a franchise that felt like a dream fit for me. Pinspiration was a new concept that was gaining momentum. The name plays off the idea of connecting the creativity of Pinterest and combining it with an opportunity to create projects full of personal inspiration.

I liked the idea of having a franchise to help guide me through the process of starting a business. They assisted with finding resources for real estate, marketing, web, and basic operating structure. I teamed up with an incredible group of talented people across the United States, all diving into this exciting opportunity together.

I sold the idea to my husband, and with his support, we jumped into entrepreneurship. We named the parent company for this new project, Of Course You Did, Inc. We signed a lease and started construction in January 2020, with a Grand Opening planned for March 2020. What could go wrong?

While I could easily outline the challenges we encountered entering a high-touch business at the same time as the pandemic, what matters most has been the personal journey that I am fortunate enough to share.

The act of following a dream is more personal than anything I have felt in business. As a leader, I often take a personal approach, but this was different. Every decision I made impacted the livelihood of my family and the families of my team. I wanted to be proud, but I had a balance sheet in front of me that told me differently. My leadership story is that of resilience, tenacity, and drive, but the duration of this experience outstretched all of my signature strengths. I began to feel that I was losing my identity.

For 20 years, I identified as a high-level leader with a list of challenging success stories. Carrying that weight as a measure of my value into this section of my life was not helpful.

The feeling of losing my identity was a result of diminishing confidence and my swagger along with it. My "swagger" is my shield that keeps me going through obstacles. Digging deeper are the parts that come together to create this shield: thoughtfulness, creativity, outspokenness, confidence, accountability, and deep compassion.

Within this five-year period, my life drastically changed. My job and my income suffered. I lost my dad. I was in a car accident that resulted in a long-lasting concussion. I had multiple challenges with raising two boys, all while trying to build a high-touch small business during a pandemic.

For every challenge, we have a choice. I will not begin to undermine how difficult it is to make any choice when the challenges stack up. However, what I learned about myself is that I had all the tools I needed, but this time, I needed to use them differently.

My first tool was me. My creativity, my ability to problem solve, and the knowledge behind business growth. The pandemic of 2020 fell in the month of my planned soft opening. The world shut down, but the expenses did not. I had to think quickly to be able to keep my team employed and to hold on tight to all the work that had gone into the business thus far.

Families were staying home, kids were out of school, and parents were learning how to multitask in new ways. That's when the idea came about to make art kits for students. I began reaching out to schools within a 15-mile radius. We came up with unique canvases and step-by-step instructions that would allow kids to create a masterpiece within the comfort of their own home.

To make this appealing for the schools, I provided a fundraising opportunity with the PTOs. In each kit, we included a pamphlet of our business that beautifully displayed our offerings. As the climate changed and the world opened up, these students ended up being the first groups of kids who hosted birthday parties and signed up for summer camps.

My most creative effort came from social media. I often put together tours of the studio, short videos of our projects, and photos of the safe way we were conducting business. I started following local news anchors and TV personalities on social media. I used tools such as Facebook and Instagram to comment on stories and tag them on fun projects we were doing in the studio.

After many attempts, I received a message back from a local daytime show that wanted to showcase some of our projects. This grew into a valuable partnership. I pitched a recurring segment on the show, and we were able to film remotely a series of projects that mirrored the in-studio experience.

Over the years, this show has visited our studio multiple times. The partnership we grew was mutually beneficial, but more so pivotal in maintaining our ability to stay open during very challenging times. I will always be grateful for the anchor that took a risk on my small business.

My second tool was my amazing team. As an entrepreneur, each experience a customer receives related to your business is an extension of you. Customer joy becomes your pride, customer disappointment is your failure. Choosing a team is the absolute extension of how you want to be represented.

While I held a passion for event planning and crafting, I will admit I am not the most skilled artist. These were skills I needed to hire. I envisioned this studio as the place where everyone feels welcome and safe to create projects that make them smile, laugh, and enjoy the company of their family, friends, coworkers, and teammates. This meant that my team needed to be talented, friendly, and have the ability to teach and multitask. We needed to have fun with people and maintain order, as customers are literally throwing paint at one another in our Splatter Room. (The room where you get dressed up in protective gear and throw paint on a canvas while simultaneously getting it all over your friends and family. There's even a glow-in-the-dark option!)

My team checked all the boxes. I have met and worked with some of the most incredible women throughout this experience. Their connection to our customers created important events such as birthdays, anniversary celebrations, team building, proposals, gender reveals, bachelorette parties, and life celebrations.

The studio's finances struggled from the setbacks around opening. To ensure my team was taken care of, I had to forgo paying myself. This led to the decision to go back to work as I knew it before. I found a great job and found myself working throughout the week for my new employer and then all weekend at the studio.

This became very tiresome, and the people who were impacted most were my two boys. Soon after I made this change, I was in a car accident that left me with a concussion for several months. While I was lying in bed recovering, I received a phone call that my dad had become very ill. Life had just delivered a very specific line of feedback, and I knew that I had to make some changes.

My team stepped up in ways I could have never imagined. These women were no longer artists; they had become customer service agents, leaders, and business owners. They stepped in and took on most of the major responsibilities for me so that I could be who I needed to be.

I was there almost every day for my Dad's last few weeks of life. We shared conversations, and he got to experience a fully present and committed daughter because of what my team did for me. I will never forget how meaningful this was to me. I will never forget the way they showed up for me to take care of myself and my family. These amazing women even showed up for me at his funeral.

This leads me to my most profound tool: my friends and family. My husband and my boys have shown undeniable support from the beginning. Despite the change in income and the increase in working hours, we found ways to connect as a family. Idea sharing around business drivers became a fun activity we could do together.

During our first summer being open, the Chamber of Commerce held a concert series. The concerts were lined with local businesses in booths. My husband and boys showed up alongside me each week to create fun activities for the shows. We made time for each other while connecting to the community. Our family vibe helped to entertain both parents and children during the shows.

Even through the hardest of months, my husband offered words of encouragement and support. His trust carried me through some of my most challenging identity struggles.

Asking for help has been an ongoing battle throughout my personal and professional life. While I am quick to support and listen to others, I often hesitate to ask for the same in return. Fortunately, I learned something new throughout this experience. Allowing friends and family to be there for me, to help me, was just as much about them as it was about me. Allowing people to support me on something so personal showed a reciprocal level of intimacy and trust to those who truly care about me. I accepted help for hiring my team, building out my space, marketing, painting canvases, and modeling projects. My family and friends were the first to hold parties at the studio and sign their kids up for projects and camps.

My mom stepped up repeatedly for everything and anything. She even broke out of her comfort zone and painted some canvases for me. They are two of my absolute favorites that will always be in my personal collection. Above all else, she remained my trusted advisor. The person who reminded me when to be proud and challenged me when my balance was misaligned.

Some of the brightest gifts in times of change come from your advisory board. I have heard this referenced in leadership talks, books, and business, and that's because this team of people is completely instrumental in personal success. People need their people. I need my people. I have friends that I have worked with for years that I call my sponsors. They objectively encourage me through feedback and always support me in rooms I am not in. They want what is best for me and will do all they can to keep me on the right path both personally and professionally.

I have girlfriends who know that sometimes I need someone around to sit quietly with when my social battery goes low. I have amazing friends who know that the best conversations don't have to end with advice but simply a judgment-free ear.

I have a family that helped pick up the pieces that I would usually carry, but couldn't. The depth of that support was immeasurable.

Through entrepreneurship, I am reminded that I can think outside of the box. My creativity is a force and a unique ability full of value. I learned that, despite what people have told me, everything I touch does not turn to gold. My reputation is a result of my tenacity to make the hard things look easy. Understanding the difference builds my character.

I am proud of the fact that I took a risk on hiring a team of artists, knowing that I would have the business acumen behind it. I helped this team realize who they were not only as artists but as businesswomen, too. Together, we built their confidence, résumés, and skills.

I found my amazing network of family, friends, and colleagues who support me no matter what I choose. Through this journey, I truly learned that being a wife, a mom, a leader, a business owner, and being a truly committed friend are not mutually exclusive, but rather they are the sum of all the parts of who I am. I may have started off wondering how I got here, but five years later, I have come to realize this was exactly where I am meant to be!

Amanda Wibbenmeyer is the owner of Pinspiration Chesterfield. Pinspiration is a do-it-yourself arts and crafts studio that specializes in creativity for all ages through events, parties, and projects located in Chesterfield, Missouri.

In addition to becoming an author and owning her own business, Amanda is a retail leader overseeing store locations throughout Missouri, Illinois, and Iowa. As a member of the G.R.I.T. community, Amanda enjoys networking, mentoring, participating in panel discussions, and public speaking engagements. She earned her Bachelor of Science degree from Loyola University Chicago.

Amanda and her husband Mike have been married for 20 years. Together, they have two boys, Andrew and Alex. As a family, they enjoy traveling to landmarks, amusement parks, and participating in scouting events.

Please scan the QR code to connect with this author.

RESOURCE LISTINGS

gritgrowthresilienceintentiontenacity.square.site

G.R.I.T. empowers individuals to lead through personal and professional Growth, Resilience, Intention, and Tenacity. When we share our stories, we encourage leadership, establish a legacy, and ensure a lasting impact.

G.R.I.T®
GROWTH RESILIENCE INTENTION TENACITY

---

adonis-itad.com

Adonis ITAD delivers secure, sustainable IT asset disposition, ensuring compliance, data protection, and eco-friendly recycling for businesses, maximizing value and minimizing risks.

Adonis
ITAD & E-WASTE RECYCLING

Keeping your date and the environment secure.

WelcomeToUndivided.com

Undivided Wealth partners with individuals and families to simplify complexity, align wealth with values, and provide clarity, confidence, and direction for a life well-lived.

UNDIVIDED
WEALTH MANAGEMENT

Transforming lives well beyond money.

RESOURCE LISTINGS

teambravohome.com

Guiding buyers and sellers through every step of their real estate journey with concierge-level service, expert negotiation, and nationwide connections. Combining a trusted team approach and personalized care.

TEAM BRAVO

Saint Louis' Real Estate Home Team

tai-chiconsulting.com

We empower organizations to achieve balanced, sustainable growth through strategic guidance, mindful leadership development, and holistic approaches that drive meaningful change, resilience, and long-term transformation.

TAI-CHI
CONSULTING

Human Resource Solutions to Grow Your Business

duvari.com

We're a people-first IT staffing firm that goes beyond hiring — we help shape culture by building teams with clarity and purpose.

duvari
Listen·Connect·Guide

RESOURCE LISTINGS

exit11coffee.com

Visit one of our Missouri drive-thru locations for specialty coffee, organic house-made syrups, energy teas, and breakfast. Get freshly roasted beans shipped to your door. Exit11Coffee.com

Cultivate Real Connections through Stellar Service, a Happy Hustle, and Carefully Crafted Coffee

---

gitzellfairtrade.com

A BIPOC woman-owned importer and wholesalers of handmade African home décor at the intersection of fair trade and smallholder farming with a mission of Improving livelihood.

Improving the livelihood of families in Africa

---

djohnsonpaintingllc.com

D. Johnson Painting is a minority-owned painting company trusted by top contractors and institutions across the region. We have earned our reputation through integrity, detail-driven execution, and a passion for giving back.

RESOURCE LISTINGS

archfordcapital.com

Dedicated to providing comprehensive guidance for wealth, legal, and accounting — all in one place. Intentional communication and advice to preserve your legacy and family harmony.

ARCHFORD®
Taking Care of Families™

---

engagementoring.com

Engage Mentoring helps companies prepare future leaders by providing mentoring and coaching programs for leaders and high potential employees that deliver results.

engage
mentoring
Prepare your future leaders

---

nwoitservices.com

NWO IT Services is your trusted technology partner, providing Managed IT Services with a team of experts ready to help when you need it most.

NWO IT SERVICES
We are your technology partner.

189

RESOURCE LISTINGS

alliance-technologies.co

Most IT providers patch issues. We drive business results. Alliance Technologies helps your business regain control of technology with managed IT, cybersecurity, and project support.

IT solutions that work for people

RREnvPartners.com

We are Environmental, Health, and Safety consultants providing extensive knowledge, experience, and expertise to assist you with a broad range of EHS needs and challenges.

R&R ENVIRONMENTAL
PARTNERS, LLC
Your Partners in Environmental, Health, and Safety
